The

FIRE

of the

WORD

The
FIRE
of the
WORD

MEETING GOD ON HOLY GROUND

CHRIS WEBB

FOREWORD BY RICHARD J. FOSTER

An imprint of InterVarsity Press
Downers Grove, Illinois

InterVarsity Press
P.O. Box 1400, Downers Grove, IL 60515-1426
World Wide Web: www.ivpress.com
E-mail: email@ivpress.com

InterVarsity Press® is the book-publishing division of InterVarsity Christian Fellowship/USA®, a movement
of students and faculty active on campus at hundreds of universities, colleges and schools of nursing in the
United States of America, and a member movement of the International Fellowship of Evangelical Students.
For information about local and regional activities, write Public Relations Dept., InterVarsity Christian
Fellowship/USA, 6400 Schroeder Rd., P.O. Box 7895, Madison, WI 53707-7895, or visit the IVCF website at
<www.intervarsity.org>.

Scripture quotations, unless otherwise noted, are from the New Revised Standard Version of the Bible,
copyright 1989 by the Division of Christian Education of the National Council of the Churches of Christ in
the USA. Used by permission. All rights reserved.

Page 26: Incredulity of St. Thomas, 1602-03 (oil on canvas) by Caravaggio, Michelangelo Merisi da
(1571-1610). Schloss Sanssouci Potsdam, Bradenburg, Germany/Alinari/The Bridgeman Art Library. Used
by permission.

Page 97: Photograph courtesy of the author.

Page 177: Rublev's famous icon showing the three Angels being hosted by Abraham at Mambre: Alex
Bakharev/Wikimedia Commons

While all stories in this book are true, some names and identifying information in this book have been
changed to protect the privacy of the individuals involved.

Design: Cindy Kiple
Cover images: Morey Milbradt/Getty Images

ISBN 978-1-61793-614-2

Printed in the United States of America ∞

For Sally

"Fy chwaer a'm priodferch,
yr wyt wedi ennill fy nghalon,
wedi ennill fy nghalon ag un edrychiad."
Caniad 4:9 (BCN)

CONTENTS

FOREWORD

The *Fire of the Word* is a marvel and a joy. How thrilling to welcome this fresh, new voice to the field of Christian spirituality. Chris Webb has accomplished what few have succeeded in doing; he has given us courageous openings onto what a life hid with Christ in God can be like. As I read this book, I felt the words on the page calling out to me, inviting me into a deeper, fuller way of living . . . a way of living that is joyfully creative and soul-expanding. The more I read, the more I felt my heart burning within me, a little like those disciples on the road to Emmaus (Lk 24:32). How do I name the feeling? What should I call it? Perhaps I could describe it as an open invitation into "The Order of the Burning Heart."

Let me share with you three compelling reasons for reading *The Fire of the Word*.

First, this book is saturated with grace and mercy. The stories, the teachings, the allusions, the very feeling tones of the words themselves are soaked in grace and mercy. Grace and mercy given in good measure, pressed down, shaken together, running over.

Chris writes, "From the first chapter of Genesis to the last chapter of Revelation, the Bible jubilantly proclaims *grace* to this world; an exuberant, life-embracing grace that exceeds anything we could possibly hope or imagine."

Chris, however, is doing far more than simply using words of grace and mercy. He, for example, does substantial theological work to cut through the Gordian knot of the common juxtaposition of the Old Testament God of wrath and the New Testament God of love. His work here is impressive indeed.

Second, this book gives us a deep sense of reverence and awe before the majesty of Scripture. Chris gently leads us before the wonder of Scripture where "the boundary between heaven and earth has been worn through." In another place he describes the Bible as "a thin place through which the presence of God breaks into this world and bursts with unpredictable consequences into our lives. Even though it is not consumed, this book burns with unquenchable fire." With exuberant flair he writes, "the inspiration of Scripture is something greater, something wholly other: a life and presence has been breathed into Scripture. . . . The Bible contains . . . the divine Author himself. Here the voice of God is heard; but God not only speaks, he makes himself fully present—gentle as the still small whisper on the mountain, terrible as an army with banners—breaking through the pages into our hearts, our lives, our world."

For all his exuberance over Scripture, however, Chris is careful not to fall into worshiping the Book—bibliolatry as we say. He knows that the purpose of the Bible is to lead us into an adoring love of the triune God—Father, Son and Holy Spirit. Worship belongs to *Yahweh* alone.

Third, this book gives us insights into faith-filled living that often surprise us, pleasantly so. Chris's stories surprise us: the tortured art work of Caravaggio, the soaring poetry of Ann Griffiths, the incredible devotion of three monks in a tiny Order called the Little Brothers of Nazareth, the determined search of Mary Jones for a copy of the Bible. And more. Chris's phrases and metaphors surprise us: he describes pride as "the all-consuming black hole of the soul"; he says of the Bible that "fire is trapped under the ink"; he reminds us that "sinners may have the wildest parties, but saints have the most fun." Drawing on an ancient Christian tradition, Chris's reinterpretation and use of the Song of Solomon surprise us.

Personally, the high point of the book, and a pleasant surprise, came with Chris's theological work on the medieval thinker John Duns Scotus. That is a name with which you may not be familiar, but by the time you finish this book, you will not only know his name but have a clear understanding of how important he is to our whole understanding of Christian spirituality. Chris's analysis of Duns Scotus's concept of "the absolute primacy of Christ" with its multi-layered implications for the work of spiritual formation is simply masterful!

I commend to you *The Fire of the Word*. It is a book which will both teach and delight. *Tolle, lege*—take, and read.

Richard J. Foster

1

HEAR HIS VOICE

❧

It's just a little before six in the morning and the alarm on my cell phone is ringing. It's winter, and the air in the room is cold and sharp; I grab a warm sweater as I stumble out of the bedroom and head down the stairs. The house is quiet, the family asleep; I'm reminded of some words of the sixteenth-century Spanish poet and mystic John of the Cross: "One dark night, fired with love's urgent longings—ah the sheer grace!—I went out unseen, my house being now all stilled." On this dark morning, my home silent around me, I'm heading into the gloomy basement, flashlight in hand, fired by those same urgent longings. It's time to pray.

Some while back I converted a corner of our basement into a makeshift chapel. It's a simple and rather inelegant affair: lengths of blue cloth, bought at a thrift store and pinned to the exposed rafters, form the walls, and three old rugs cover the concrete floor. A couple of yard-sale armchairs and an old bookcase provide the meager furnishings, and under the single window is a prayer desk I picked up years ago from a redundant chapel in England. On the windowsill sits a battered electric lamp, a candleholder and a wood-mounted print of the San Damiano cross before which Francis of Assisi used to pray. This is my Jerusalem, my temple: the holy ground where I encounter the presence of God.

It seemed cold upstairs, but the air down here is frigid. Shivering a little, I kneel at the prayer desk, light the candle and open my prayer book and Bible. Making the sign of the cross on my lips, I recite the traditional opening words of the liturgy: "O Lord, open thou our lips, and our mouth shall shew forth thy praise." Then, as Christians throughout the centuries have done (especially in monastic and liturgical communities), I begin the day's prayer by softly chanting Psalm 95, the great invitation to worship: "O come, let us sing unto the LORD, let us heartily rejoice in the strength of our salvation" (v. 1). And as the psalm unfolds, I absorb the poet's encouragement to sing, to rejoice, to celebrate God and his creation, to recognize his care for us.

Buried in the heart of this psalm comes a challenge: "Today if ye will hear his voice, harden not your hearts." Here is the work of today—which is also the work of the whole of life. I'm called daily to open my heart afresh to the living Word of God. I know I need this reminder but, to tell the truth, I'm daunted by the possibility that God might actually speak. I feel like an Israelite at the foot of Mount Sinai, overwhelmed by the swirling clouds at the mountain's summit, the bursts of thunder and the flashes of fiery lightning. How can I bear to hear God's voice, let alone listen to it, interpret it, comprehend it? "You speak to us," Moses was told, "and we will listen; but do not let God speak to us, or we will die" (Ex 20:19). Wouldn't hearing the voice of God be something like seeing his face: an experience so great, so consuming, that our mortal frame would be unable to contain it?

So it's with caution that, in my prayers, I approach the reading of Scripture itself. The contemporary Coptic saint Matta el-Meskeen understood this well when he wrote: "There are those who always fast to read the Gospel. There are those who, when they read the Gospel alone, always kneel. There are those who always read it with weeping and tears." The candlelight flickers as I turn the pages, and my heart trembles a little too. What will I hear? How will I be called, how changed? Will I be comforted or inspired? Or is it today that my life will be turned inside out? It has happened before—to others and to me.

Life-Changing Words

On another cold winter morning—in February of 1208—a young man named Francesco Bernardone came into a small Umbrian church to hear the mass being celebrated for the feast of Saint Matthias. For three years Francesco had been living as a hermit in the Spoleto Valley under the direction of a community of Benedictine monks. The son of a wealthy cloth merchant, he had become estranged from his family and many friends because of the eccentric fervor with which he seemed to be seeking God's will for his life—emptying his father's warehouse to provide for the poor, caring for outcast lepers by washing and redressing their wounds, and begging from house to house as he raised money to rebuild local churches.

As the mass ended and the little church began to empty, Francesco approached the priest. He quietly explained that hadn't understood the Gospel reading (which would have been in Latin); would the priest kindly read through it again? The cleric obliged, taking Francesco through the passage from the tenth chapter of Matthew's Gospel line by line. He translated Jesus' words about the apostles traveling from place to place curing the sick, raising the dead and ministering to lepers (that last part must have caught Francesco's attention). Jesus told them to journey without money or baggage, and to trust in faith that God would provide through those among whom they went. Above all, they were to proclaim the heart of the Gospel message: "The kingdom of heaven has come near!"

As he listened to the priest's explanation, Francesco's heart began to race; he could sense the calling of the Spirit on his own life. "This is what I want!" he cried. "This is what I seek! This is what I desire with all my heart!" From that moment on his course was set: Francesco would become a wandering preacher, an itinerant proclaimer of the kingdom. He would travel in poverty and faith to the furthest reaches of his world, throughout Italy and on to France, Germany, Spain, the Balkans, even to northern Egypt to share the good news of Christ with a Muslim sultan who was facing a great European crusading army. Francesco's shining example of obedience to the gospel would become legendary, inspiring generations of Christians until the present day. Francesco is known to us as that startling lover of Christ, St. Francis of Assisi.

Scripture not only sparked Francis's tremendous spirituality, it continued to fuel the burning flame of his passion for Jesus. By 1210 the rapidly growing Franciscan movement had caught the attention of the wider church, and Francis was encouraged to present a community rule to the pope. The text of that rule no longer survives, but it seems almost certain that it was little more than a collection of sayings of Christ from the Gospels. That spirit was reflected in the opening words of a revised rule he composed a decade later, in which he committed himself and his Friars Minor ("Little Brothers") simply to "follow the teaching and footprints of our Lord Jesus Christ." Francis had experienced the Bible (especially the Gospels) as a life-changing book and was determined to stay open to its transforming influence.

His experience was far from unique; similar stories could be repeated from every age of the church's life over the last twenty centuries. Almost a thousand years before Francis, Antony of Egypt was a young farmer and landowner in the Upper Nile region. One Sunday morning as he walked into the traditional Coptic service in his local church, he heard the priest reading from Matthew's Gospel: "If you wish to be perfect, go, sell your possessions, and give the money to the poor, and you will have treasure in heaven; then come, follow me" (Mt 19:21). The impact was striking and immediate. Antony sold everything and retreated into the Egyptian desert, charting a course which would be followed later by thousands of others who were seeking a deeper and more committed life with God. The *Life of Antony*, a short biography by the Alexandrian bishop Athanasius, touched the lives of Christians and churches across the Middle East and Europe, and helped lay the foundations of the monastic movement; Antony himself is often known as the "father of monasticism." And all this grew from that unexpected encounter with the words of Scripture.

A little over fifteen centuries later, in the remote Welsh village of Pontrobert, the young daughter of a local farmer became captivated as she listened to the Calvinistic Methodist preachers whose fiery sermons were lighting up the pulpits of Wales. She soaked herself in the vivid scriptural imagery which permeated their teaching, and began to sew together a patchwork of metaphors, symbols and allegories into one of the most striking collections of hymns and poetry that Welsh culture has ever known. In every line the impact of the Bible on her life and faith is glaringly evident. One of her hymns, *Bererin llesg gan rym y stormydd*, opens with this verse (in English translation):

> Pilgrim, swept by storms and weary,
> raise your head, look up and see:
> Jesus, Lamb of God, our Savior,
> clothed in robes of majesty;
> girdled with the gold of loyalty,
> round his hem the bells ring clear,
> singing grace to every sinner:
> Christ, the eternal Yes, is here!

Remarkably, this single verse ranges across almost the whole

sweep of Scripture as it references Paul's experience of being shipwrecked in the Mediterranean (Acts 27:13-44), John the Baptist's
exhortation to "Behold the Lamb of God!" (Jn 1:29 KJV), John the
Evangelist's vision of Jesus on the island of Patmos (Rev 1:13),
the clothing of the Levitical priests (Ex 28:33-35) and the story of
the woman reaching for the hem of Jesus' garment (Mt 9:20-22).
Into this are woven theological allusions to the incarnation
(Christ's vestments symbolically reach to the earth) and the atonement. It's a remarkable synthesis for a young woman who lived
and worked on a rural sheep farm and had only a rudimentary
education to her credit.

These poems and hymns, now considered treasures of the
Welsh language, might have been lost to us altogether after Ann
Griffiths's tragic death at the age of twenty-nine, had they not been
collected by her maid and published in the early nineteenth century by Thomas Charles of Bala, a clergyman living over the
mountains in northwest Wales. Around the time of their publica-
tion, Charles was also playing a key role in an initiative which
would enable countless others to experience the life-changing
power of Scripture for themselves. At the turn of the century a
young teenager named Mary Jones turned up at Charles's home,
having walked twenty-six miles, barefoot, across the Welsh mountains. She had been saving money for six years and had made her
difficult journey with one purpose: to buy a Bible.

Charles was impressed and shaken by her single-minded determination and her passionate hunger for Scripture. A couple of
years later he related the story to friends meeting together in London, and lamented the scarcity of affordable Welsh-language
Bibles which could be distributed to those, like Mary, who longed
to read Scripture for themselves. The friends decided to create an
organization to translate, publish and distribute the Bible as widely
as possible—and so the British and Foreign Bible Society was
born, the first of the many Bible societies throughout the world,

which have made Scripture available and accessible to millions.

In our own time we might consider the life of Martin Luther King Jr., a moral and political leader whose speeches and example changed the face of Western society. The catalysts of the civil rights movement are well known: the arrest of Rosa Parks on a Montgomery bus for refusing to give up her seat for a white man, the longing of so many to see integration in the public school system, the desperate circumstances of many black Americans in the southern states—to name just a few. Less often acknowledged, though, is the direct role of the Bible in shaping King's life and actions. The inspiration for his nonviolent resistance came directly from the message of Jesus (and, of course, from the example of Gandhi, but Gandhi in turn frequently acknowledged his indebtedness to the teachings of Christ). King looked particularly to the Sermon on the Mount, where Jesus spoke of turning the other cheek and loving our enemies. His teaching about "creative suffering" was rooted in his reading of the Passion narratives. And his astonishingly inclusive social vision, expressed so movingly in the legendary "I have a dream" speech, was grounded in the Gospels, where Jesus is continually presented as the friend of all those on the edges of first-century Jewish culture—sinners, tax collectors, women, lepers, outcasts. In every way, King was a man changed and shaped by hearing the voice of God.

All these remarkable figures from the history of the church relived, in one way or another, the formative experience of Moses standing before the burning bush. Most of us are familiar with the story. Moses, having fled Egypt after murdering one of the Egyptian slave drivers, found himself herding sheep in the stark, rocky desert of the Sinai peninsula. Day after day he wandered the trackless wasteland, moving the flock from one watering hole to another; a former prince of Egypt, he had become a forgotten solitary in the wilderness, invisible to the rest of the world—as though already dead.

From time to time small brush fires would spark in the dry, brittle undergrowth, but one day Moses was surprised by crackling flames in the branches of one of the desert bushes. The fire appeared to be burning vigorously, but the bush was not consumed by the flames. Intrigued, curious, perhaps a little afraid, he clambered over the rocks to get a closer look. As he drew near he was astounded to hear a voice from the fire calling to him. "Come no closer!" he was told. "Remove the sandals from your feet, for the place on which you are standing is holy ground" (Ex 3:5). By this point Moses was trembling with fear, aware now that he had somehow stumbled right into the presence of God.

During the conversation which follows, Moses received the word of God, a sort of condensed Scripture. The range of material covered in these few paragraphs of text is remarkable and encompasses most of the key themes and genres of the biblical text in abbreviated form. There are promises: "I have observed the misery of my people who are in Egypt . . . and I have come down to deliver them" (Ex 3:7-8), and there are commandments: "I will send you to Pharaoh to bring my people, the Israelites, out of Egypt" (Ex 3:10). These affirmations and instructions are set in the context of God's dealing with his people in history ("The LORD, the God of your ancestors, the God of Abraham, of Isaac, and of Jacob, has appeared to me" [Ex 3:16]) and theological reflection on God's character and nature ("'I AM WHO I AM.' . . . 'Thus you shall say to the Israelites, I AM has sent me to you'" [Ex 3:14]). God performs miracles, challenges Moses' reticence, gives him prophetic words, rebukes him and reveals something of a future yet to come. There are even a couple of poetic lines in verse 15 as God shares his name with Moses: "This is my name forever, and this is my title for all generations." God's words to Moses are almost a Bible in miniature.

The experience of meeting God at the burning bush changed

Moses. Despite his uncertainties and doubts, his weaknesses of character and his fears, his life was turned around from this point forward. Emerging from his desert hiding place, he confronted one of the mightiest leaders of the ancient world, led an entire people out of slavery and through forty years of nomadic desert wandering, stood atop Mount Sinai in the midst of fire and thunder to receive the Torah from God, with whom he spoke face to face, and became one of the most significant figures in world history. His experience in the wilderness changed him, changed those around him and ultimately transformed the world.

But the most significant aspect of this entire experience was not the words that Moses heard. It was neither the history nor the theology, not the wisdom or the poetry. Moses was not changed by a text. He was utterly transformed by a direct encounter with God, an experience which was mediated through the words. When Moses heard the voice of God, he shook with terror and hid his face in the folds of his robe. Why? Because he was about to receive a couple of chapters of the book of Exodus? No! He was awestruck because the voice he heard made real and immediate the presence of the Holy One of Israel. In the words, Moses met God. And so can we.

As I kneel in my cold chapel this morning, I read these words in the dim lamplight: "A voice cries out: 'In the wilderness, prepare the way of the LORD'" (Is 40:3). I'm learning to listen for that voice in Scripture, the cry that summons me to be ready for God's presence. It's the voice of the prophets and the seers, the patriarchs and the priests. It's the call of the wisdom chasers, the evangelists, the poets, the apostles. It is the cry of the Bible from beginning to end: Maranatha, "Our Lord, come!" (1 Cor 16:22).

So then, the invitation to us is this: not to explain God but to experience God. Kneel alongside me, and we'll listen for his voice together. We are on holy ground.

Readings

At the end of each chapter of this book are readings that will help you explore the theme of the chapter more fully: seven readings for each chapter, enough for a week of meditation and reflection. If you follow this course of prayerful experience of the Bible alongside your reading of the book, you will spend almost four months learning to read and pray with Scripture in a fresh and enlivening way. That's enough time for the practices described here to become habitual and second nature. Your reading of the Bible will have been transformed.

These first seven readings are intended simply to provide a gentle starting point. Each reading describes a biblical encounter between an individual and God's word. Some are a little strange (for example, John eating a scroll), some involve hearing God speak directly (as with Moses), and others with God's Word being read (such as Jesus in the synagogue).

Spend a little time with each of these, reading them through slowly and prayerfully. Ask God to use these readings to help you understand both how Scripture has affected the lives of others and how it affects your life. Ask the Spirit for insight into your relationship with God through the Bible. You may want to journal or make notes you can return to as you work through the remaining chapters of this book. After finishing the book and undertaking all the suggested reading exercises, you could review your notes from this first week to see how your experience of God in Scripture is being transformed.

Day 1	Exodus 3:1-7	(Moses hears the voice of God)
Day 2	1 Samuel 3:1-10	(Samuel hears God in the temple)
Day 3	2 Kings 22:3-20	(Josiah rediscovers the book of the law)
Day 4	Nehemiah 8:1-12	(Ezra reads the law in Jerusalem)
Day 5	Psalm 119:33-48	(the psalmist rejoices in the law)
Day 6	Luke 4:16-22	(Jesus reads in the synagogue)
Day 7	Revelation 10:1-11	(John consumes God's word)

2

LEARNING TO READ AGAIN

The filthy Roman backstreet was wrapped in darkness. Foul-smelling water trickled between the stones underfoot, and a single guttering candle burned in a window high above. A drunken young man, his clothes tattered, stumbled into a doorway and threw up violently. Across the street two prostitutes, their faces garishly painted, cackled with delight as they watched him slide down the doorframe and fall into the pool of his own vomit. He looked up sharply, and they noticed the angry purple bruise forming around his left eye. Yelling a colorful curse at them he tried to clamber to his feet but slipped and fell again. Howling with laughter they turned the corner and disappeared.

He sat in the gloom for a couple of minutes, staring up at the flickering candle, lost in his hazy thoughts. Then he pulled himself to his feet again and weaved his way toward another doorway at the end of the street. He hit the door hard with his shoulder and it crashed back on its hinges, toppling him into the inky blackness of the hallway beyond. Cursing and groaning, he clattered noisily up the wooden staircase; a voice from a neighboring house yelled at him to keep quiet. Pushing open another door, he tumbled his way into a large attic studio and collapsed into a chair in the middle of the open floor. The candle, now burning low, sat in the open window behind him. As the light shone over his shoulder, he contemplated the canvas mounted on the easel before him. There were four figures gathered in a tight huddle in the center of the painting, surrounded by a thick and impenetrable gloom. Their faces were illuminated by some bright light, but everything else lay in darkness. For perhaps half an hour the young man pondered before the canvas, unmoving, his eyes half shut; a casual observer might have thought him asleep.

Then, with a start, he leaped up and frantically began mixing paints onto a cracked wooden palette—thick, oily purples and browns, grays and greens. Stabbing a brush into the mixture, he began edging color into the shadows around the leftmost figure. He painted for hours, energetically, even frenetically. As dawn began to color the city in a soft crimson light, the painter, now somewhat more sober but utterly exhausted, fell back into the chair and examined his work thoughtfully. He closed his bloodshot eyes and nodded. It was finished.

On the canvas, three disciples stood in a tight group around the newly resurrected Jesus. Matthew and John looked on in wonder as an incredulous Thomas pushed his finger into Christ's wounded side. Jesus, his eyes etched with compassion, held Thomas's wrist, keeping the hand steady. The scene was shocking and extraordinarily tender all at once. Without doubt a masterpiece.

In his chair, Caravaggio slept.

The Language of Art

A few years ago I had the opportunity to hear a seminar given by Neil MacGregor, the director of the British Museum who had formerly worked for fifteen years as director of the National Gallery in London. He had been asked to speak about the relationship between faith and art. Despite MacGregor's impressive reputation, though, I didn't come into the seminar with high expectations. Visual art had never been a language I'd felt able to understand. When I took a stroll around a gallery (a rare enough event in itself) I never found myself able to get beyond an instinctive "that looks good/terrible" response; as for what the artist was trying to say, and what the significance of the work might be more widely— how should I know? In the end, was there really any more to it all than the creation of attractive pictures and sculptures to fill up empty spaces?

MacGregor held me spellbound for an hour. Never once did he lecture to the experts (You know: "This, of course, is an ironic reversal of neoclassicist assumptions"). Instead he spoke to the philistines, like me, who knew little and appeared to care even less. We looked together at examples of early Christian marble carvings and compared them with a contemporary sculpture fused together from impounded rifles in Africa. We lingered over Pieter Brueghel's *Christ and the Woman Taken in Adultery*, losing ourselves in the darkness and shadows. MacGregor gently showed how the use of color here or texture there contributed to some sense and meaning, some story or idea. And together we discovered how all this expressed and deepened the way people thought about life, faith and God. I came away feeling somehow expanded, enlarged.

And I was hungry. I bought and borrowed books of paintings. I started looking for opportunities to visit the galleries I'd formerly ignored. The paintings on the walls hadn't changed; the same mixtures of pigments hung on the same old canvases. Still, something was different. Now, for me, this art had a voice. I saw Salvador Dali's *Christ of Saint John of the Cross* in Glasgow and was overwhelmed by its immensity and power. On a visit to London I made time to see an exhibition of Botticelli's drawings for Dante's *Divine Comedy* and was enraptured for hours. I even had a framework with which I could appreciate some of the stranger expressions of modern art, which before had been incomprehensible; I spent an entire afternoon captivated by the collection in the Saatchi Gallery alongside the Thames.

Then I discovered Caravaggio. My introduction to this early Baroque genius was through his painting *The Incredulity of Saint Thomas*, a work he completed in the midst of a life of riotous drinking, womanizing and brawling in the first year or two of the seventeenth century. He was an unlikely biblical interpreter, but someone had, perhaps, neglected to tell him that only saints were allowed to encounter God in Scripture. *The Incredulity* is a passionate and moving painting. Jesus and three of his disciples stand with their heads almost pressed together; the apostles' faces are etched with astonishment as Thomas's finger slides into a sliced fold of flesh in Jesus' side. Caravaggio was pioneering a vividly realistic and naturalistic style, and the sheer *physicality* of the work is palpable; he shows the resurrected Christ as a solidly flesh-and-blood man, brutally pierced by the nails and yet living and breathing still.

Caravaggio, *The Incredulity of Saint Thomas*

Of course, this is precisely the point of the biblical story which so captured Caravaggio's imagination. The Gospel of John tells us that when Jesus first appeared to the disciples after the resurrection, one of their number was missing. The other disciples had faithfully gathered in the upper room, but Thomas was wandering somewhere in the darkness. And when he hears later of this appearance of the risen Christ, he cannot bring himself to believe it—in fact, he bluntly refuses to accept it. Did Caravaggio, the drunken, violent reprobate, see something of himself in Thomas? The outsider, the misplaced doubter, the one who was never in the right place when God showed up?

But John's narrative continues:

A week later his disciples were again in the house, and Thomas was with them. Although the doors were shut, Jesus came and stood among them and said, "Peace be with you." Then he said to Thomas, "Put your finger here and see my hands. Reach out your hand and put it in my side. Do not doubt but believe." (Jn 20:26-27)

This is the moment Caravaggio seeks to portray. Little wonder that his painting is so graphic; the biblical text itself is shocking. I have read a dozen expert commentaries on John's Gospel since first discovering Caravaggio's work, but none have come close to conveying the sheer emotional impact of this scene with anything like the immediacy of that oil-smeared canvas.

Whenever I look at this painting, really see it, allowing myself to be drawn into it as MacGregor has taught me, I find the experience intense and overwhelming. The darkness surrounding the figures holds my gaze on that tightly packed group, the horrific wound, the probing finger, the startled eyes. I feel short of breath. I have been opened to the power of art.

My world has changed. Someone has taught me to read.

The Master of Paradox

This book is also about learning to read. Most of us, if we're going to experience the Bible as a life-changing text charged with the presence of God, are going to have to learn all over again how to read it. There are all sorts of assumptions and preconceived ideas we may need to lay aside, and some new expectations we'll need to nurture. There are fresh skills to be learned, the skills of attentiveness, openness and obedience rather than (or, more correctly, alongside) the skills of the linguist, the exegete and the theologian. Learning to read again will be like learning anything else: it will take time and practice; there will be frustrations and setbacks; we will need to apply ourselves in a sustained and dedicated way.

Much of what I write in these pages is the fruit of my own explorations, guided by the wisdom of the great Christian thinkers and writers of past ages. Of course, my life (probably rather like yours) is lived out on a rather smaller canvas than the great figures we looked at in chapter one; I am no Francis of Assisi or Antony of Egypt—and certainly no Moses. Still, I've shared something of their experience: meeting God on the holy ground of Scripture has also changed my life—repeatedly. This ancient book has spoken into my contemporary world with startling clarity and irresistible authority. It has guided crucial decisions, shaped my moral universe, molded my worldview and constantly challenged my assumption that, as the poet W. E. Henley put it, "I am the captain of my soul." I wouldn't be living where I live, doing the work I do, surrounded by the people who make up my world—in fact, I wouldn't be the person I am today—if it weren't for the way the softly insistent voice of Christ has spoken to me through the pages of Scripture.

By the time I reached my early twenties I was investing a lot of time and energy exploring spirituality. I wasn't a complete stranger to the Bible or the Christian faith; I'd been very keenly involved in a church youth group in southern England in my teenage years.

But by that point my spiritual odyssey had taken me in a very different direction: I was a faithful practitioner of Zen meditation. I devoured Buddhist and Taoist texts. I invested long hours trying to master the basic breathing and concentration techniques. I struggled against the incessant flow of thought in search of the "empty mind." And I waited. There is a teaching in Zen that you don't seek a *roshi*, a spiritual master, to teach you the way to enlightenment. You simply practice your meditation and, when you are ready, your master will find you. So, patiently, I practiced and watched for his coming.

While I waited, a friend gave me a book of koans to use in my meditation. A koan is a sort of Buddhist riddle, an insoluble puzzle designed to force the mind to think beyond its normal parameters, to push itself beyond rational thought into the realm of intuition—a classic and well-known example is: "What is the sound of one hand clapping?" But many traditional koans don't work well in a Western context; they're too culturally inaccessible, rooted in the thought world of ancient China and Japan. The book I was lent tried to address that by gathering together a series of well-known paradoxical sayings Westerners could relate to more readily. It was a collection of the sayings of Jesus from the Gospels.

Jesus, of course, is the master of paradox. "Those who try to make their life secure will lose it, but those who lose their life will keep it" (Lk 17:33). Or try this: "The last will be first, and the first will be last" (Mt 20:16). Jesus encourages people to abandon their wealth in order to find great riches. He calls them to give that they might receive "a good measure, pressed down, shaken together, running over" (Lk 6:38). He tells his followers that he has come that they might have "life, and have it abundantly" (Jn 10:10)—and then summons them to take up a cross and follow him to death. After two thousand years of diligent preaching, we think we have a pretty good handle on his parables, but those who first heard them were left confused and bewildered; even his own disciples often had to ask for an explanation. Is it all that surprising, then, that even Buddhists find themselves admiring Jesus as a teacher whose message pushes the mind beyond its usual limits?

So, armed with my new book, I began to meditate on the Gospels. I immersed myself in the sayings of Christ. I turned them over and over, day and night, hoping to be overcome by their strange internal logic. I wandered into a church and started going to a small group where other people were reading and thinking about his words. And, in the end, the inevitable happened. I had been waiting for my master, and my Master found me—he just wasn't the master I expected. I heard the call of Christ through those words of the Gospels, and my world was turned upside down.

I still experience the Bible as the great koan of my life. For me, these words find their fullest meaning not solely in themselves but, beyond that, in the encounter to which they lead. I find myself coming to Scripture the way an Orthodox worshiper approaches an icon. To those of us more familiar with the conventions of classical Western art, the stark outlines and vivid colors of these sacred Byzantine paintings seem to create an air of strangeness, otherness. The longer we look into them, the more we realize that their perspective appears all wrong: the lines of buildings and tables don't converge toward the far horizon as we expect, and the proportions and postures of the people can seem awkward, even strained. At first, everything seems confused.

But as we look longer, we are struck by the sudden realization that the angles and postures are all perfectly natural and correct—or, at least, they would be if we were dwelling in the world of the icon. But we are not. We are outsiders, looking in on the kingdom of heaven: it is our viewpoint that is distorted. To look into an icon is to be challenged to reconsider our perspective, to discover a new place to stand where everything falls into correct alignment, to be invited to step through into an alternative reality: the reality of God's kingdom.

Like an icon, and like a koan, the Bible comes to every one of us as something wholly strange and unusual, a world sketched out in awkward and irreconcilable angles. It alternately comforts and jars, inspires and grates. Scripture is untidy, unwieldy, difficult. We stretch our minds to make sense of it—categorizing, systematizing, shaping everything into neat theological compartments. Yet the Bible resists us at every turn. It will not cooperate, it will not conform to our schemas, it will not be tamed. But then, of course, Scripture does not seek to be analyzed and understood. The Bible is not a theological textbook, a philosophical treatise or the answer book to life's questions. It is a thin place through which the presence of God breaks into this world and bursts with unpredictable consequences into our lives. Even though it is not consumed, this book burns with unquenchable fire.

A Blunted Blade

If we're honest, though, we don't always experience the Bible as a dramatic and powerful force in our lives. Most people, after reading the Gospels, don't go and sell all their possessions and devote themselves to a monastic community or a life of itinerant preaching like Francis and Antony. Nor does Scripture always seem to crash into our imagination the way it did for Ann Griffiths, soaring through her soul and bursting out in poetic ecstasy. And long before the ministry of Martin Luther King Jr., throughout the decades leading up to the American civil rights movement, the Bible had been widely read and discussed, but it hadn't caused many people to reshape their views on justice for African Americans or other minority groups. In fact, in previous generations the Bible had been vigorously used to defend slavery and the subjugation of the "sons of Ham" (that is, people of African descent).

The Bible clearly has the potential to provoke the most radical and far-reaching changes in individuals, societies and nations. And yet equally clearly, the Bible is read day after day by countless numbers of people, and shared Sunday by Sunday in millions of churches around the world, without that change being widely experienced. The Word of God may claim to be "living and active, sharper than any two-edged sword" (Heb 4:12), but for many of us the edge of this sword seems to have been dulled, and its capacity to pierce our hearts and souls somehow blunted. It's not hard to find people who know the Bible well, intimately even, and yet seem to be largely untouched by its message.

A friend recently told me the story of his uncle who, on retirement, decided to read right through the Bible from beginning to end in a single year. Twelve months later, having easily achieved his goal, he reasoned that with all the spare time he had on his hands, he might actually be able to read the entire book in a single month. That was a considerably more ambitious target—but he did it. And so he thought to himself, *One hundred forty-four. There's a biblical number. Now if I read the Bible once every month for the next twelve years* . . . And that's exactly what he did. Rarely has anyone been so immersed in the Bible as that man. "And here's the irony," said my friend; "my uncle died shortly afterwards . . . the meanest, bitterest son of a gun you could ever wish to meet." It's the tragic story of too many Christians and churches: soaked in Scripture, yet in the end completely untouched.

Sometimes, of course, the reason is very simple: resistance. We don't want to be changed. As soon as the Bible begins to challenge us, to undermine our prejudices and dogmas, to call for a change in our lifestyle and priorities, then the shutters slam down. Changing the world would be fine. But changing my life is not part of the deal.

But resistance—which we all experience to some degree—is only part of the picture. Many of us would welcome an encounter with Christ through the pages of the Bible. We come to it with a longing to meet with God. We know that meeting may not be easy; we may, like Jacob, end up wrestling with God in the dark night until, beaten and exhausted, all we can do is cling to him and refuse to let go. But we are so deeply dissatisfied with ourselves and our lives, so sharply aware of the pain and fury of the world around us, and so keenly aware of our utter inability to do anything about it, that we are more than ready to take the risk of opening our lives to him.

When we start rustling those thin India-paper pages, though, something else happens. Maybe the words of Leviticus ("On the eighth day he is to take two lambs without blemish, an unblemished ewe one year old, three-tenths of wheaten flour mixed with oil for the oblation . . .") begin to wash over us until our minds slumber. Or we turn to Paul but are unable to hear his voice without also hearing the echo of preacher after preacher who has taken his breathless vision of life in Christ and turned it into a neat little system with compartments and categories for everything. Perhaps miracles spring from the page to confuse us (*Did this really happen? Is it wrong to ask that question?*). The big picture may elude us, so that we find ourselves disoriented by the confusing parade of kings, prophets, judges, seers and priests. There are parts of the biblical story that (rightly) shock and outrage us: murder, rape, genocide, often justified in God's name. How are we to understand these stories, and how should we respond? And on top of all this, many of us struggle with the Bible simply because we've been taught over and over how to mine this book to extract truth, but rarely how to open ourselves to it so that we might come face to face with the living God.

It doesn't have to be this way. It is possible for us to experience the unpredictable sharp edge of Scripture. The Bible retains its power to act as a koan, an icon, a meeting place between earth and heaven. It has the inbuilt capacity to thrust us into the presence of God. We just need to rediscover how to read it.

Readings

The seven readings below are koans drawn from the teaching of Jesus. Some are outright paradoxes (losing your life in order to save it), while others are puzzling and obscure (no one is greater than John the Baptist, who is least in God's kingdom).

It's very tempting to dodge the force of these sayings by trying to wrestle a straightforward solution out of them. As you read and reflect this week, try not to succumb to that temptation. Don't avoid the difficulty of these words: live with it. We're trying to open ourselves to a new way of reading in which we don't have all the answers—there may not always be answers to be had—but we are content to stay present to the text as it makes us present to the great and eternal mystery of God.

Again, recording your response to these readings, both your thoughts and your emotional reactions, may be very helpful; you can come back and review these notes after completing the book and reflect on how your practice of reading may have changed or grown.

Day 1	Mark 8:34-37	(save your life by losing it)
Day 2	Mark 9:33-37	(the first must be last)
Day 3	Mark 10:41-45	(the greatest must be a slave)
Day 4	Matthew 10:34-39	(not peace but a sword)
Day 5	Matthew 11:11-15	(John the Baptist, the greatest and least)
Day 6	Luke 17:5-6	(great faith like a tiny seed)
Day 7	John 12:24-25	(life comes through death)

3

DO NOT BE AFRAID

The old university lecture hall was a little decrepit; paint was peeling off the mildly damp walls, and the harsh fluorescent lights overhead mercilessly exposed every crack and chip in the wooden seats and desks. But the Christian Union had worked hard to brighten the mood, and it showed. Colorful bunting had been hung from one side of the room to the other. A green embroidered cloth hung over the speaker's podium. The coffee was fresh and the doughnuts warm. We were encouraged to find a seat while three cheerful musicians played and sang brightly. One of the senior students welcomed the speaker who, he said, had a gift for sharing the good news about Christ in a compelling and attractive way. The preacher thanked him, stood and slowly surveyed a room filled with faithful and heathens—members of the Union, and others (like me) invited to come and discover "what life is *really* all about." He sized us up carefully before looking down at his notes.

"Sin is a serious business," he began quietly, his deep gravelly voice taking on the tone of a schoolteacher about to give his class a real dressing down. "I wonder if you realize just how serious it

is? How terribly serious a matter it is to be a sinner?" He looked up,
his penetrating eyes trying to peer into the soul of each one of us
in turn. Picking up his Bible, he began to read from Paul's letter to
the Romans:

> There is no one who is righteous, not even one;
>   there is no one who has understanding,
>   there is no one who seeks God. . . .
> Their throats are opened graves;
>   they use their tongues to deceive.
> The venom of vipers is under their lips. . . .
>   There is no fear of God before their eyes. (Rom 3:10-11,
>   13, 18)

He fixed upon us with his steely eyes again, before launching into
a blistering denunciation of every sin we could ever have imagined,
and a few that appeared to come as surprising news to some of the
more innocent students in the room. He excoriated the filth of sin,
he condemned the depravity of vice, he lambasted the hubris of
every wretched man, woman and child who dared offend the holiness of God with their base wickedness. We sweated with guilt over
everything we had ever done, even some things we hadn't dreamed
were sins before that night—but, after all, wasn't even our righteousness nothing but filthy rags? It seemed we couldn't do anything right;
when we were bad, we were evil; and when we were good, we were
so unclean we polluted even our attempts at virtue. For forty-five
minutes he held us squirming while hell gaped under our chairs.
And then, quite suddenly, he stopped. And, incredibly, he smiled.

"But I have a wonderful message for you, my friends!" he
chirped. "There is hope!" We leaned forward onto the edge of our
seats. Surely this must be the good news we had been promised at
the beginning of the evening? After that excruciating diagnosis of
our dreadful spiritual condition, we were anxious not to miss a
word of the remedy.

"Christians," he said, "have developed a marvelous vocabulary to describe this hope, this good news. Words like *atonement. Propitiation. Justification. Sanctification. Glorification.*" He smiled. "Oh, my friends, these words sum up the wonderful hope of the Christian. These words express the glorious gospel of Jesus Christ. These words are balm to the soul!" His gaze, now entirely enraptured, drifted upward toward some seventh heaven. "Oh, my friends," he sighed, "you really should learn for yourselves what these words mean!"

He was silent for a moment. Then he picked up his notes and sat down.

A little while later I mumbled an excuse to my friend and crawled out of the room. I had no idea what any of those mighty and glorious words meant, and they drifted off into some airy far corner of my mind. But the preacher's vivid denunciation of the evils of sin stayed with me for days. Whatever else you might want to say about God, this much was clear: God is mightily ticked off. With the world. With humanity. And especially with me.

An Uncertain Love

In this book we're exploring how Scripture might become for us holy ground on which we can meet God, be drawn into his presence. But, of course, this implies that we *want* to draw near to God. And the simple truth is that, while we might be very willing to hear God, obey God and worship God, many of us are deeply reluctant actually to draw near to God, to open ourselves to the possibility of his divine embrace, because we are so very uncertain of God. After all, we are such wretched sinners. What would a holy and righteous God want with us? Or make of us? Or *do* to us?

Of course, we understand that God loves us. We have heard the love of God proclaimed in a hundred sermons. We have memorized the Scripture verses: "For God so loved the world . . ." (Jn

3:16) and "God is love" (1 Jn 4:8). We have sung God's love in hymn and chorus; we have reassured one another over coffee in church that "God loves you!"; we have plastered affirmations of the love of God on our Bible covers, our car bumpers, our pencils and fridge magnets and toothbrushes. We know that God loves us.

And yet . . . and yet many of us cannot quite believe it. Our mind affirms it, but something deep in our heart questions it. When we look at ourselves in the mirror, we don't always like what we see. Even if we have hidden our flaws, our failings and our weaknesses from others, we cannot hide them from ourselves. We are painfully aware of the inner struggle with those secret vices we would never dare to name in public. There is a darkness within, a shadowy alter ego we keep firmly locked away. We may have succeeded in hiding our true nature from those around us, at least to some degree. But we are unable to hide from ourselves. Nor can we hide from God, the "Father who sees in secret" (Mt 6:4). He is the one, as an ancient prayer expresses it, to whom "all hearts be open, all desires known, and from whom no secrets are hid." How could this all-knowing God desire our company, our friendship?

And so we find ourselves understanding and affirming the limitless love of God on the one hand, yet on the other living as though God's love were actually rather more measured and circumspect—in fact, barely more than grudging indulgence. Our hearts tell us that we are sullied. Spoiled goods. In the presence of a holy and pure God we are filthy and contaminated, an unpleasant irritant, a bad odor. Any grace God extends toward us is, we feel, surely against his better judgment. We tell one another that God loves us, but our hearts tell us that God tolerates us.

Our lives demonstrate this reality. Our relationship with God is driven around a never-ending cycle of remorse: our failings and faults lead to guilt; guilt to alienation, the shattering of our friendship with God; alienation to sorrow and abject confession; confession to glorious restoration, often with extravagant promises to ourselves that *now* we will break the cycle, that this must never happen again; but in the end, with seeming inevitability, we prove unable to fulfill those heartfelt sacred vows and we plunge back into the morass of our faults and failings once more.

Our ability to experience intimacy with God, to practice his presence, comes to depend entirely on where we find ourselves in that cycle. When we feel morally whole, living in that spiritual sweet spot where prayer comes easily and worship is pure delight, then God draws close and we walk together joyfully. But when we fall, we fall into darkness. God seems to retreat, perhaps in disgust. Prayer turns to ash in our mouths. Guilt wraps its black tendrils around our souls. We are sucked into a cloying mire, a slow and sorrowful drowning of the spirit, until desperation drives us (or grace prompts us) to throw ourselves once more on the mercies of God. Again we come back, again with the same confession, the same failures, the same broken vows. Will he really forgive this time? Can the great rift between us be closed yet once more?

We ride this emotional and spiritual rollercoaster because of the image of God we carry in our hearts: a loving Father when we behave, but a pitiless judge when we stray. As long as we allow such an image to remain festering in our souls, we will always find it difficult to experience the intimate presence of God through Scripture—or, indeed, in any other way. If we believe that God truly has such a jaundiced view of us, we will never be able to accept that he might welcome our company. We will be unable to draw near to him, because in our hearts we are not sure he wants us to draw near; he is holding us at arm's length, always responding to our attempts to draw closer by pushing us a little further away. Such a heart image of God is the death of intimacy in prayer.

But of this we must be certain: God is not so.

Surprised in San Diego

My own experience of this kind of turbulent relationship with
God, alternating between closeness and guilt-laden separation, is
direct and personal. For years I struggled to become the kind of
person with whom I thought God might desire intimacy: someone
devout, holy and pure. But throughout that time (and, of course,
right to the present) I wrestled daily with the particular vices that
disordered my soul, my thinking and my behavior. We all have
such besetting faults, I believe, although in each of us the toxic
mix is slightly different.

I have something of an addictive personality, so my worst vices
include lust and gluttony, with an unhealthy side serving of wrath
from time to time. I have always found it difficult to establish
good, appropriate relationships with women. Unable to cope with
my wayward desires I tend to resist intimacy of any kind, making
it difficult to lay the foundations for friendship. I have learned to
recognize in my impatience with others the seeds of the anger I
too often allow to boil away under the surface and sometimes fail
to restrain. And gluttony pulls me toward overindulgence—with
more than just food.

One morning in my early twenties I fumbled around the kitchen
making coffee. I was already halfway through the first cup of the
day before it dawned on me that I had dosed it with a liberal help-
ing of cheap brandy—just like every morning for some time now.
Like someone waking from a bad dream, I went over to my heavy
overcoat and pulled the small bottle of whiskey from the inside
pocket. In a moment of awful clarity I realized where this road
was leading. I wasn't an alcoholic—not yet, at least. I knew I hadn't
tumbled over that precipice, not quite. But I was so close. Terri-
fied, I tossed out the bottle, poured the coffee down the sink, and
set out to learn the art of sobriety. Since then I've walked with others as they've battled chronic drinking problems and seen the
fearsome struggle it entails. I had a lucky escape.

Paul compared himself with other sinners and found himself to be the foremost and worst in that company (1 Tim 1:15). Like many I have often found myself usurping that title in my own estimation. Every time my vices prevail, I vow never to be overcome again. Yet every time I rise up from the dust only to fall once more. The pattern is depressingly predictable. It so often seems that my so-called desire for holiness is no more substantial than the morning mist, burned away by the first heat of temptation. And though I say that I fall, the truth is that often I jump. I indulge my vices, humor them, enjoy them. I am, in my eyes, the chief of sinners.

How could God love such a person? Some time back I found myself squarely confronted by that question as I prayed with Scripture. For seven months I was engaged in the Spiritual Exercises of Ignatius of Loyola (which we'll explore in more depth in chap. 9). During the first few weeks of the Exercises I was encouraged to reflect on passages of Scripture which, in one way or another, speak about the love of God, the joy of embracing that love or the seriousness of refusing it.

During this time I had to travel to San Diego. One morning I found myself on a hotel room balcony, coffee in hand, enjoying the cool, restful air of dawn and reflecting on that day's passage of Scripture. My spirit was drawn, as it had been many times over the previous few weeks, into these words of John's first letter: "By this we will know that we are from the truth and will reassure our hearts before him whenever our hearts condemn us; for God is greater than our hearts, and he knows everything. Beloved, if our hearts do not condemn us, we have boldness before God" (1 Jn 3:19-21). My heart often condemned me before God; I had been wondering what it might mean for my heart to be reassured. My thoughts circled around the passage for some time without finding any resting place.

After a while, my mind began to wander. Below my balcony an annex of the hotel jutted out abruptly, its rooftop spattered with throbbing air conditioning units. Dirty, oily water pooled in the corners of the flat roof, and a rusty ladder led down the back of the building. It was an ugly sight, in vivid contrast to the scenery beyond—gracefully arching palm trees; warm, burned-orange adobe buildings; and radiantly bright bird of paradise plants. The juxtaposition of such beauty with the stark, functional inelegance of the hotel's backside was startling. Daydreaming, I began to imagine the people living in the houses I could see around the hotel, people who were also both beautiful and ugly, wonderful and depraved, corrupted and magnificent all at once. Everywhere I looked I could either see, or vividly picture, a world grim and glorious in equal measure. I wondered: when God looks at this world, its filth and its brilliance, what does he make of it? Could God love it, this ruined perfection?

And then I heard the voice of God, or at least a whisper of it. I should mention that for me this was extremely unusual, as I believe it would be for most people. I've met a very few folks in my time who seemed to have a genuine mystical gift enabling them to hear God's voice frequently, and I've often wondered what that might be like. But whenever I've sought God's specific guidance about some issue, I've had to content myself with the more normal experience of feeling God's gentle nudging in a particular direction or a vague intuition of something God might be trying to say. And even those moments are few and far between. I do often enjoy a very strong sense of God's presence, for which I am deeply grateful, and which makes possible a richer enjoyment of contemplative prayer. But actually hearing God's voice? I could count on the fingers of a single hand the number of times I'm sure I've experienced that in over twenty years of Christian discipleship.

This was one of those moments. The voice of God came, clear and compelling. A gentle word spoken from afar and heard deep within: *It is what it is, and it is wonderful.*

I carefully put down my half-drunk mug of coffee; my hand was shaking. I stood for a moment, breathless, alert. I could hear that voice echoing in my soul: *It is what it is, and it is wonderful.* For what seemed like the first time I understood—really understood, somewhere in my heart, my bones, my guts—that God loves this world. This wild, disordered, amazing, pain-wracked, elegant, sometimes incomprehensible world is, above all else, loved by God. His heart is woven through it and wrapped around it. He loves not only what it was or what it could be, but above all what it is, right now. "God is greater than our hearts," John had written, "and he knows everything." And knowing everything, he still loves.

I am part of that world, a mirror of its confusion and corruption. I could see myself, beautiful as God had made me, and depraved as I had undone myself. And still those words reverberated within: *It is what it is, and it is wonderful.* My soul began to grasp a magnificent and awe-inspiring truth. God *knows* me, and yet God *loves* me! My vice-ridden character is unhealthy, destructive, and dangerous; neither I nor God would seek to make any excuse for that. But I had made the mistake of assuming that my moral failure defined my relationship with God, that my brokenness was the starting point (and too often the ending point) of our friendship. It is not and never will be. The realization burst in that when God looks at me, what he sees is shaped by his intense and passionate love, not by anything I may or may not have done. In my ignorance I had thought that God first and foremost wanted to deal with my sin. In reality, before all else, he wanted me.

Readings

It may be that you are struggling to experience God's love in your own life; that, like me, your opinion of yourself is sometimes harsh, and you find it hard to believe God's could be otherwise. Perhaps your friendship with God also rides the spiritual rollercoaster between highs of joyful union and lows of sin-induced alienation.

If so, I have a prescription for you, a medicine for the soul that I recommend with all my heart. I'd like you to begin immersing yourself in the Gospels. Specifically, I suggest you find every passage you can which describes Jesus coming into contact with people whose lives are troubled—the sick, the possessed, the morally corrupted, the sinful—and soak in those narratives. (Seven such passages are listed at the end of this chapter.)

Commit yourself to spending a good period of time dwelling in each narrative. First, before you read each passage, spend some time in prayer. Ask God to reveal himself to you in these words of Scripture. Open your heart and mind to the possibility of his presence becoming real as you read. Then go through the passage slowly, a few times, allowing the details of each scene to shape themselves in your mind. Try to picture the scene as vividly as you can; allow it to become real in your imagination. Be alert to the small details: the words each person speaks (and when they don't speak), actions and gestures, comments offered by the Gospel writer.

Above all, pay attention to Jesus. How and when does he speak and act? How does he seem to relate to each of these broken people he encounters? How does he treat them? Does he seem to despise or welcome them? Is he judgmental or merciful? Does he seek evidence of change in them before he offers his love, or is change a result of their experiencing his love?

Day 1	Matthew 8:5-13	(a Gentile centurion)
Day 2	Matthew 9:9-13	(Matthew the tax collector and his friends)
Day 3	Mark 1:40-45	(a leper in Galilee)
Day 4	Mark 2:1-12	(a paralyzed man lowered through the roof)
Day 5	Mark 5:21-43	(a woman healed and a girl raised)
Day 6	Luke 5:1-11	(fishing with Peter and his companions)
Day 7	Luke 7:36-50	(a woman in the home of a Pharisee)

4

THE YEARNING OF GOD

It might be well to pause at this point. For me, that spiritual experience in San Diego was powerful and enduring. It reshaped my soul at the deepest level and continues to affect my life and prayer right into the present. Hardly a day passes, even now, without my reflecting on that moment. But even our strongest and most significant spiritual experiences—including those which are rooted in our meditation on Scripture—must constantly be held up to the light of the biblical texts. Of every experience we must be ready to ask: Is this consistent with the experience of God witnessed in Scripture? Is it in harmony with the understanding of life before God which the Bible describes? Are there any jarring discrepancies between my experience and biblical teaching?

The answers, in this case, are not immediately obvious. After all, doesn't the Bible seem to paint two rather conflicting portraits of the character of God? First, there is the God of law, judgment and wrath: the God who thunders from the fire on Sinai, who writes immutable law into tablets of stone, who strikes down sinners with earthquakes or plague, and who is ready to send an entire nation into bitter exile as a punishment for their infidelity. Second, we have the God of love: the God who forgives, who is merciful, kind and gentle, who is willing to endure the suffering of the cross for the sake of his people. And if we reconcile these two images, don't we end up with the picture of God described earlier—alternately welcoming us in his mercy and condemning us in his anger, torn between the impulse to love and the fiery drive to maintain purity and holiness?

We'll look again in chapter ten at the way we can approach the Old Testament as a book of grace and love. For now, let's fix our attention on Jesus, in whom we can most clearly see the character of God made manifest.

Holding the Broken Ones

Never once, in any of the four Gospels, do we find Jesus holding broken, contaminated and soiled people at arm's length. Quite the opposite: he embraced them. He was known as the "friend of . . . sinners" (Lk 7:34). He often overwhelmed people's reticence and fear with the sheer intensity of his desire for friendship and intimacy. The Gospels are replete with stories of people drawn into Christ's presence despite themselves, despite their failings and inadequacies, their foolishness or moral bankruptcy. Take, for example, the story of Zacchaeus.

Zacchaeus was a senior tax collector in Jericho, almost certainly despised by the local community as a treacherous collaborator with the occupying Roman forces. By his own admission in the Gospel narrative, he collected not only the required taxes but also a healthy "bonus" of his own on top. He cheated, defrauded and grew rich on the backs of others. When Jesus came through Jericho, the Gospel tells us (Lk 19:1-10), Zacchaeus found his curiosity piqued: he wanted to see this famous rabbi for himself. But, Luke says, "on account of the crowd he could not, because he was short in stature. So he ran ahead and climbed a sycamore tree to

see him." We might justifiably wonder whether the tree also provided a convenient hiding place, a leafy blind from which he could
spy out Jesus without being seen himself.

Jesus was not fooled. As he passed under the tree he looked up,
catching Zacchaeus's troubled gaze. And then Jesus said something quite remarkable: "Zacchaeus, hurry up and come down; for
I must stay at your house today." The Greek text of the Gospel is
very strong here; the words "I must stay" are forceful, as though
Jesus were under some kind of irresistible compulsion. What was
that driving impulse? An instinct that this would be a significant
moment for Zacchaeus? A command from his heavenly Father? A
need to make some important theological point? Any of these are
possible. But I believe the compulsion was something rather
deeper. Jesus was impelled by his yearning for Zacchaeus. Like
the persistent father scanning the horizon for any sign of the
prodigal son, Jesus looked into the branches of that tree and saw
one for whom his heart longed. The Song of Songs expresses the
moment well: "I found him whom my soul loves. I held him, and
would not let him go" (Song 3:4).

Why does that seem the most likely explanation of Jesus' words?
Because of the way the rest of the story unfolds. Consider for a
moment: what is it that brings about Zacchaeus's dramatic conver-
sion? What enlightening spiritual teaching does Jesus give? What
moral challenge? What call to renewal of life? What is the crucial
word which Jesus speaks?

Jesus says nothing. Nothing, that is, beyond the words he has already spoken: "I must stay at your house today." He walks home
with Zacchaeus. They dine together. We have no record of their
conversation. They may have discussed the significance of prophecy in salvation history or compared theories of the atonement. Or
they may have argued agreeably about sports, lamented the recent
poor weather or swapped jokes. It hardly seems to matter. We
need to understand this: Zacchaeus did not stand up and an-

nounce the transformation of his life because of some striking point Jesus made during the dinner conversation. Luke would scarcely have missed the chance to record one of Jesus' great sayings. No, Zacchaeus was turned inside out simply by being in the presence of Jesus. He discovered that his brokenness and depravity were no barrier to the love of God. If Jesus had told him, "Zacchaeus, only amend your life and God will take such joy in you!"— well, such a message Zacchaeus might have believed easily, even as it drove him to despair. But Jesus told him something quite different, and not in words but in action. Zacchaeus, God *delights* in you. God yearns for you and longs to be with you. Right now, messed up as you are, God is impelled by love to draw near. Zacchaeus, I *must* stay with you today.

As John is so keen to remind us, "God is love" (1 Jn 4:8). The image of God we see in Jesus is consistent with the picture presented throughout Scripture. And it is possible to encounter this marvelous, loving God in Scripture. We are capable of drawing near to God, of experiencing God in our lives. Scripture itself assures us that God wants us to draw near, longs for our companionship and friendship. God yearns for us.

Behold the Man

I cradled a cup of hot coffee in my hands as my friend wept over Scripture. Sitting in the back room of a church during a break in a conference, I was listening to Juanita Rasmus talk about the Gerasene demoniac while traffic hummed on the freeway beyond the window. Juanita and her husband, Rudy, pastor St. John's Downtown, a Methodist church in Houston which includes significant numbers of homeless people, alongside others who for one reason or another have found themselves right out on the edges of the community: folks with AIDS, with mental health issues, with addictions—the list seems endless. Just lately this Gospel story had been playing through her head with a peculiar resonance.

She crossed the room, pulled a Bible from a scuffed bookshelf and found the passage:

Then they arrived at the country of the Gerasenes, which is opposite Galilee. As Jesus stepped out on land, a man of the city who had demons met him. For a long time he had worn no clothes, and he did not live in a house but in the tombs. When he saw Jesus, he fell down before him and shouted at the top of his voice, "What have you to do with me, Jesus, Son of the Most High God? I beg you, do not torment me"— for Jesus had commanded the unclean spirit to come out of the man. (For many times it had seized him; he was kept under guard and bound with chains and shackles, but he would break the bonds and be driven out by the demon into the wilds.)

Jesus then asked him, "What is your name?" He said, "Legion"; for many demons had entered him. They begged him not to order them to go back into the abyss.

Now there on the hillside a large herd of swine was feeding; and the demons begged Jesus to let them enter these. So he gave them permission. Then the demons came out of the man and entered the swine, and the herd rushed down the steep bank into the lake and was drowned.

When the swineherds saw what had happened, they ran off and told it in the city and in the country. Then people came out to see what had happened, and when they came to Jesus, they found the man from whom the demons had gone sitting at the feet of Jesus, clothed and in his right mind. And they were afraid. (Lk 8:26-35)

"These are the people who come to our church," Juanita said quietly, tears running down her cheeks. "Driven from one place to another, unwelcome everywhere, ragged and weighed down in chains. They're just a problem to everyone else. Somewhere along

the line they just stop being human beings and start being a nui-
sance, a problem to be solved, a complication to be dealt with.
They're tormented wherever they go." She looked up at me, her
eyes filled with sorrow. "How many times had this man been
crushed?" she whispered. "Even when Jesus arrives, all he can
imagine is that he's about to get hurt again."

I picked up the Bible and looked again at the familiar words,
reading them as though for the first time. I could see the man,
fallen to his knees, pulling his filthy rags tight around his body for
security. I saw the look of desperation in his eyes. *What do you want
with me, Jesus?* he sobbed. *Are you here to torture me—just like everyone else?* I thought back to the year I had spent working in a church
of the homeless in southern England, remembering the addicts,
drunks, prostitutes and broken souls who had stumbled into our
doors. Their haunted faces were still vivid in my memory; the feral
caution they had shown when they first arrived, a suspicion born
on the hard streets.

In all the times I had read this passage I had never felt the man's
pain so immediately and sharply.

Juanita was still talking quietly, her hand resting gently on the
page. "And look what he does," she said, pointing to the line where
Jesus asks, *What is your name?*

For a few years I had helped coordinate meetings of my de-
nomination's Deliverance Ministry Team, a group of clergy who in
a former generation would have been known as exorcists. Now I
realized, as I looked at the words under Juanita's fingers, that I had
probably spent a little too long among them. I'd read the books
and heard the talks; I'd been told that this story illustrates the way
Jesus was careful to identify the precise nature of a spiritual afflic-
tion before taking action. Naming the demons gives you power
over them—whether the "demons" are rapacious spiritual beings
or simply metaphors for deep psychological issues.

But now I was reading afresh, and I saw that Jesus wasn't speaking to these evil spirits. He wasn't interested in the demons. Luke is very clear: Jesus spoke to the *man*. This man, who had been tortured and tormented by all around him, expelled from the community, left wrapped in his own darkness among the tombs— Jesus wanted to know who he was. When the demons spoke for him, Jesus simply pushed them aside. Jesus was looking intently into this man's heart and soul, perhaps the first person ever to do so, and he was asking, *Who are you?*

I was no longer reading. Now I had tears in my eyes too, and I was praying. "Oh Jesus—to be loved so utterly and sought so keenly! This man was corrupted and soiled, damaged beyond repair, battered and broken. His demons had so overrun him there no longer seemed to be anything of the person left. But where everyone else saw the problem, you saw the man. My Lord! Would that I might see myself as you see me; would that I might see those around me as you see them."

Encountering Love in Scripture

Understanding that God loves us immeasurably, that he delights in us right now, as conflicted and corrupted as we are—understanding and experiencing this love is essential if we want to learn to encounter God in our reading of Scripture. It is possible, of course, to come to the Bible without this knowledge and experience. But that leads to a very different engagement with the text, an engagement that may be more damaging than helpful to our spiritual life.

We may come to the Bible convinced that God cannot love us. We are so burdened by a sense of guilt and shame that we feel completely alienated from God, certain that he casts his glowering eyes over us like a furious divine judge. Scripture then becomes a text that *condemns* us—and, all too often, a text that condemns others around us too. We find ourselves in a world of punishments and pain, a place where the threat of darkness and the gnashing of teeth is ever present. God takes joy in pouring out bowls of wrath, inflicting plagues and tightening a noose of arbitrary laws around the necks of willful sinners. The sweeping history of the Bible demonstrates a single, inevitable truth: everybody falls. At some point everyone stumbles, and God is waiting in the wings, more than ready to pounce. Scripture is a warning writ large: God is dangerous.

Of course, to sustain such a reading of the Bible we are going to need to be very selective: carefully highlighting certain passages, skating over others and putting a vicious spin on the whole. For the simple fact is that the whole tenor of Scripture stands squarely against any such understanding of God's character. The fiery preacher stands aloft in his pulpit, pounding his well-worn black leather Bible as he dooms humanity, spitting his chapters and verses on a world of cowering sinners. He can quote more of the Bible than I have forgotten; his underlinings are abundant, and his marginal notes plentiful, for he has explored Scripture thoroughly in his search for judgment. But he hasn't been paying attention. From the first chapter of Genesis to the last chapter of Revelation, the Bible jubilantly proclaims *grace* to this world, an exuberant, life-embracing grace that exceeds anything we could possibly hope or imagine. When we read this book of grace as a prescription of condemnation we have, quite literally, lost the plot. God *delights* in us. And nothing we do makes him delight in us any less than he does right now.

Alternatively, we may come to the Bible convinced that God is indeed ready to love us. All we need is to straighten out our lives enough that we might be pleasurable and acceptable to God, and he will be glad to embrace us. Scripture then becomes a text that *corrects* us. The Anglican Thirty-Nine Articles talk about reading "for example of life and instruction of manners." And indeed we can find the Bible to be a rich resource of commandments, principles, decrees, precepts, statutes and directives. We can read the swathe of historical narratives as successive acts in a great morality play, each tale with its own pointed ethical lesson for us to absorb. As the text increasingly brings our lives into conformity with God's immutable laws, so we become increasingly acceptable to him, increasingly loved.

The only problem with this approach to Scripture is that it constantly throws us back on our own meager and insufficient spiritual resources to transform ourselves. As long as we hold to the idea that if only I were different I would experience the presence of God more deeply, we find we are cornered into reshaping ourselves before God can even begin to draw near. This is the very dilemma Paul explored—and rejected—in his letter to the Romans. "I delight in the law of God in my inmost self," he wrote, "but I see in my members another law at war with the law of my mind, making me captive to the law of sin that dwells in my members. . . . So then, with my mind I am a slave to the law of God, but with my flesh I am a slave to the law of sin" (Rom 7:22-25). But Paul also rejoices in the good news of the gospel: God draws near while we are yet sinners. God already delights in us. Nothing we can do will make God delight in us any more than he does right now.

When we truly understand and experience God's delight in us, his extraordinary love for us, we find Scripture becomes a text that *captivates* us. From beginning to end it speaks to us of the deep yearning of God. We find it to be a book of love. It inspires in us a longing to be in the presence of God; it opens us to the transforming grace that heals our sin and makes us more able to experience the presence of God; it reveals the longing of God for us; it becomes holy ground on which we meet with God and consummate our love for him. It is wonderful, mysterious and beautiful—just like its wonderful, mysterious and beautiful Inspirer.

We even begin to read those dry commandments and regulations in a different light. Benedict of Nursia, the sixth-century monastic founder, expresses well the way that even law can be an

expression of love. His monastic rule is filled with directives, precepts, instructions and even recommended punishments for trans-
gressions. But the opening lines of the rule (which we'll have cause
to consider again more carefully in chapter eight) set the context
for all that follows. Benedict writes: "Listen carefully, my son, to
the master's instructions, and attend to them with the ear of your
heart. This is advice from a father who loves you; welcome it, and
faithfully put it into practice." We might easily imagine those same
words prefacing the precepts of Exodus or the prescriptions of
Leviticus.

The Jews have always understood this well, perhaps better than
Christians. We are apt to describe the first five Hebrew books of
Scripture as the "Law," a set of burdensome restrictions God im-
posed on the Israelites, who responded by trying to earn God's
favor and merit their way into glory. It's almost as though the Old
Testament was God's abortive first attempt at salvation: for centuries it was all about works, until God had a better idea on the first
page of Matthew and started toying with grace instead.

But Jews speak of these same books as the *Torah:* the teaching,
wisdom and instruction needed to live well. They see the words of
the Sinai covenant not as a dragging weight but as a gift, not the
imposition of unwelcome regulations but the grace of clear guidance for shaping a life of abundance and well-being. Christians
talk about the "Ten Commandments," but Jews about the "Ten
Words"; in Jewish tradition the first of these "Words" is not even
a commandment at all but a statement about the grace-filled foundation of God's covenant with his people: "I am the LORD your
God, who brought you out of the land of Egypt, out of the house
of slavery" (Ex 20:2). This act of liberation was pure gift, pure
grace. God called his people, God redeemed them, God set them
free, God preserved them at the Red Sea, God sustained them in
the wilderness—without any "Law." Grace, as always, came first.
This is the nature of God.

Readings

Live with these passages over the coming days. Review them often, asking God to help you see them afresh. Be focused and persistent. Stay with them until you find yourself immersed in them, until every detail becomes familiar. Memorize one or two if you are able. Turn back to them in your thoughts throughout the day—when you drive or wash dishes or walk the dog or lie in bed at night—always asking God to reveal himself through them.

As you reflect, allow the passages to become autobiographical. This is also your story. You too come to Christ as these people did. Unhealthy. Disordered. Confused. Fallen. Broken. Misused. And Christ treats you as he treated them. His words are addressed also to you. His voice is in your ears, and his touch touches you. Experience this Scripture as deeply as you can. Bathe in it. Drown in it, if you can.

I have no idea how you will experience God reading these Scriptures in this way. There is no method or system for encountering God, and no predictable result. This is not a mechanical procedure, the turning of wheels and dials to crank out predetermined answers. You may be surprised or shocked or find your world turned upside down. Pain may well up from deep within, or joy. You may be broken down or built up. It is not always easy.

But have courage. Of this one thing I am absolutely certain: if you seek God's love in Scripture, you will find it.

Day 1	Luke 8:26-39	(a possessed man thrown out of his home)
Day 2	Luke 23:32-43	(those surrounding Jesus at his crucifixion)
Day 3	John 4:1-29	(a Samaritan woman at Jacob's well)
Day 4	John 5:1-9	(an invalid lying by the pool of Siloam)
Day 5	John 8:1-11	(a woman caught in the act of adultery)
Day 6	John 9:1-11	(a man born blind)
Day 7	John 21:1-17	(Peter after his denial of Jesus)

5

MY BELOVED SPEAKS

My basement chapel is cold and dark, despite the small light of the candle flickering behind red glass on the window ledge. Yet there are other flames here; the thin pages of my Bible crackle as I turn them, as though fire is trapped under the ink. I am reminded of the haunting words of the prophet Jeremiah:

> If I say, "I will not mention him,
>> or speak any more in his name,"
> then within me there is something like a burning fire
>> shut up in my bones;
> I am weary with holding it in,
>> and I cannot. (Jer 20:9)

It seems as though somehow this book cages the same flames—but barely. Just under the surface of the words a great conflagration seethes, yearning to break out. Jesus warned us: "I came to bring fire to the earth, and how I wish it were already kindled!" (Lk 12:49). So perhaps we, who are the kindling, should be wary. Scripture is not safe. It should only be approached with the greatest caution, since every time this text is opened it has the potential to spark off the page, spread, burn and consume. The two disciples who walked with Jesus on the road to Emmaus discovered this; as they later reflected on their experience, one asked the other: "Were not our hearts burning within us while he was talking to us on the road, while he was opening the scriptures to us?" (Lk 24:32). Every time I read, then, I know I am in danger of catching fire.

The Question of Truth

This is where I must begin learning to read anew. Not with specific books or passages, nor with study guides and commentaries. What I need first is an entirely fresh perspective on the unique nature of Scripture itself.

The Bible is different from every other book, because the Bible alone is inspired—a word which means a great deal more here than we might expect. The authors of other books may have experienced some kind of inspiration, from God or from nature, from their circumstances or the depths of their own souls. Their readers, likewise, may find themselves inspired to love or rage or laughter. But the inspiration of Scripture is something greater, something wholly other: a life and presence has been breathed into Scripture, some power, some flash of the divine fire. Other books contain ideas, thoughts, concepts, dreams and visions, which may be expressed with extraordinary force or beauty. The Bible contains—or, more accurately, fails to contain, to hold back—the divine Author himself. Here the voice of God is heard; but God not only speaks, he makes himself fully present—gentle as the still small whisper on the mountain, terrible as an army with banners—breaking through the pages into our hearts, our lives, our world.

That, at least, is the theory. In practice, however, the contemporary church has managed to turn the idea of the inspiration of

Scripture into a fertile war zone. The trainers have stepped out of the ring, and two contending parties are nose to nose in a "battle for the Bible" (sadly, it usually seems to be the Bible that emerges as the prime casualty). On the one hand, liberal scholars and thinkers assert that the Bible is a collection of fallible texts that bear witness to extraordinary experiences of God, texts whose accuracy and relevance today can be questioned, tested and even fearlessly denied. But if they are right, in what sense is the Bible authoritative? At what point does it pass from being "the word of the Lord" to simply words about the Lord, which we are free to lay aside whenever they prove inconvenient?

On the other hand, conservatives affirm the divine origin of Scripture as a guarantee of its reliability and accuracy. But just how far does that accuracy extend? Is the Bible entirely utterly dependable within the realm of theology and ethics, making Scripture infallible? Or is it perhaps without error in absolutely every respect, including those times when it addresses history or science; is it, in fact, inerrant? And, in the end, does it matter? Is the divine origin and life-changing character of Scripture irredeemably compromised if, say, a man did not live in the belly of a giant fish for three days (Jon 1:17) or if Christians do not have a unique immunity to snake bites (Mk 16:18)?

Behind the conflict between these two views lies one simple assumption: that the fundamental issue at stake is whether the Bible speaks the truth. In fact, under the surface of every heated argument in today's church—including the wrangles over creation and evolution, women in leadership, homosexuality, and Christianity and politics, to mention just a few—we usually find the same three basic questions:

1. *What does the Bible say?* How does the Bible address the question at hand? What teachings, concepts and principles can we extract from the text? How are they to be interpreted? Who has authority to interpret them?

2. *Is the Bible right?* Are the principles laid out in Scripture and the assumptions on which they are built still valid today? How much of the Bible is culturally conditioned? What (if anything) in the Hebrew Bible is superseded by the New Testament or even by later developments in our theology and understanding?

3. *Is the Bible authoritative?* Even if the Bible is right, can this ancient text (and the principles extracted from it) claim our obedience? Are we called to follow the dictates of our consciences, informed by the Bible? Or are we to submit unquestioningly to this book as the word of God?

These questions are important, and I have no intention of brushing them aside. Truth, after all, is vital. Despite the philosophical and moral claims of some relativists, it is clear to most of us that we live in a structured universe that embodies absolute truths—both physical truths (the speed of light is always constant) and ethical truths (torturing children is always wrong). There are not always clear, obvious and simple answers to every issue we face—but there are often solid, knowable principles and realities that can help guide our way. Truth matters.

But the Bible is not only a book of truth—nor, for that matter, is it the only book of truth. Many books are dependable and (mostly) accurate: phone books, dictionaries, encyclopedias, to name just a few. Perhaps somewhere out in the world there is some other text which is, by good fortune, infallibly and inerrantly correct in every respect—a physics textbook, say, with no mistakes at all. What of it? Think of the ferocity of a bolt of lightning flashing across the heavens from one end to the other. No matter how reliably and authoritatively the textbook outlines Maxwell's equations for electromagnetism, reading that book is not the same as being struck by the lightning bolt. In the same way, I would suggest that when we say the Bible is inspired, we are not merely saying that it is true; we are implying so much more. What, then, do we really mean by *inspiration*?

Inspired by God

God began inspiring before a single word of Scripture was ever written. The second chapter of the book of Genesis tells the story of creation and the shaping of the first human being: "In the day that the LORD God made the earth and the heavens, . . . the LORD God formed man from the dust of the ground, and breathed into his nostrils the breath of life; and the man became a living being" (Gen 2:4, 7).

Here is the very first act of *in-spiration*, in-breathing. God takes a handful of earth and shapes a clay mannequin, human in appearance but lacking the divine spark, and into this being he breathes his own life. Thus the man becomes a "living being"; not just biologically animated, like the animals, but filled with the vibrant spiritual life of God himself. Inspired in this way, human beings have the "image" and "likeness" of God (Gen 1:26); in some way, the life and presence of God are made incarnate in the physical universe through these "in-breathed" creations.

It is almost certainly this passage of Scripture that Paul had in mind when he reminded Timothy that "all scripture is inspired by God" (2 Tim 3:16). Paul's language is particularly rich and vivid here; he coins a new Greek word, *theopneustos*, which literally means "God-breathed." The picture this word paints is striking. Imagine God taking ink and molding it, shaping it into line after line of elegant, mysterious symbols, ribbons of Hebrew, Aramaic and Greek. He traces these lines across papyrus scrolls and parchment sheets, ordering and aligning them, drawing them together into tales from long ago, tearful laments, joyful cries, deep pools of wisdom and philosophy, and so much more. Then he binds together the whole into a single huge, meandering, delightful tome: the Bible.

It is an astounding book, a book of marvels. The poetry soars, the stories sing, the prophecies rattle the soul. This book has a breadth and depth any other author could only dream about. And yet . . . and yet, it is still just a book, a collection of words pinned to paper and stitched into a cover of black leather. It is wonderful, but it is not enough. God is not simply an author of texts—he is the Author of life. And this book is not to be *theographos*, God-written; it is to be *theopneustos*, God-breathed.

So God does more than bind truth, insight and wisdom into the words. He breathes the words out from within and somehow binds his own Spirit into the book. And just as the man became a living being, so this book becomes "living and active" (Heb 4:12), the "living and enduring word of God" (1 Pet 1:23). This is why Moses implored the Israelites to "take to heart all the words that I am giving . . . the words of this law," because they are "no trifling matter for you, but rather your very life" (Deut 32:46-47). Jesus likewise impressed on his disciples that "it is the spirit [or "breath"; the Greek word is the same] that gives life. . . . The words that I have spoken to you are spirit and life" (Jn 6:63).

This is inspiration. Life breathed in. An expression in this material creation of the essence and presence of God. A space where the image and likeness of God can be found, experienced and encountered. A place where the boundary between heaven and earth has been worn through. When we open the Bible, the key question is not whether this book is able to give us reliable, authoritative truth. The more fundamental issue is whether we are able to endure and embrace God, who will meet us face to face on the holy ground of these pages. When we open the Bible, it does not say to us, "Listen: God is there!" Instead, the voice of the Spirit whispers through each line, "Look: I am here!"

How the Heart Sings

We struggle to read the Bible as an inspired book, though, because many of us have been taught to come to Scripture in a very particular way: the way of the theorist.

As theorists, we have learned to treat the text as an object of

study, something to be decoded, analyzed and understood. Paul
wrote to Timothy that he should be "rightly dividing the word of
truth" (2 Tim 2:15 KJV); many of us in the contemporary Western
church have perfected the art of clinically dissecting it. In studies
and classes, books and sermons, we have discovered how to lay
Scripture on the laboratory table and slice texts into tiny constitu-
ent atoms, teasing out layer upon layer of meaning as we work.

For theorists, the Bible represents an enormous intellectual
challenge, a complex equation of almost limitless terms. Once we
begin to study in earnest, we realize that so many variables come
into play: the original languages; the cultural context; the process
of composing, editing and transmitting the writings; the interplay
between various texts and their authors; the process of communi-
cation and interpretation involving author, text and reader; historical uses of the texts—the fields of study are endless. As a result, lengthy papers can be (and are) written about a single word
in a single verse. Page after page can be consumed exploring, for
example, how a certain Greek word was understood in antiquity,
in the ancient Greek translation of the Hebrew Bible, in the New
Testament, in Paul's theology, in the writing of the early church—
and all this before anyone even begins to consider what the word
might mean in the context of a particular verse or paragraph or
book of the Bible.

But at some point such scholarship becomes not merely exhaus-
tive; it is simply exhausting. The life and soul of the book being
studied is crushed under the weight of commentary. Even the
most ardent scholar, walking through the aisles of a theological
library and perusing mile after mile of such detailed study en-
tombed in dusty journals and voluminous tomes, might perhaps
be tempted to recall the advice of the Teacher in the book of Ecclesiastes: "Of making many books there is no end, and much study
is a weariness of the flesh" (Eccles 12:12).

The theorist aims for mastery of the text. But such mastery is elusive. There is always more to study, always more to learn. Every answered question raises a dozen more, and as quickly as solutions are grasped, just so quickly do they run through the fingers. In the meantime, theorists discover that the end result of aiming to master the Bible is always the same: it dies in our hands.

There is, however, another way: the way of the lover. A lover does not seek to master the Bible but rather to be seduced by it. True lovers do not despise academic study of Scripture; after all, who would not want to discover secrets that help them know their beloved more intimately? No, good scholarship is precious to the lover. But for the lover, study can never be an end in itself; rather than rejecting study, a lover seeks to go beyond it. When we read the Bible as lovers, we are not aiming simply to understand Scripture, to interpret it, to draw from it a coherent framework of teachings and truths that help make God, life and creation comprehensible. We do not come primarily seeking moral and ethical principles, theological insights, or even practical life applications. We come to be kissed by Christ.

The young woman in the Song of Songs cries out: "Let him kiss me with the kisses of his mouth!" (Song 1:2), and this is also the cry of the lover of God who opens the pages of Scripture. Speak, Lord! Come, Lord Jesus! Make this place, this book, "the house of God" and "the gate of heaven" (Gen 28:17). Let my reading of these words become a tryst between us, an intimate encounter, an embrace. Again, does this mean we despise scholarship and study of the text? Not at all. May we be allowed, as Paul expresses it, to "understand all mysteries and all knowledge" (1 Cor 13:2). But not without love, not without fire, not without being brought into his presence. Oh, let him kiss me!

The Voice of My Beloved

It might help to illustrate the distinction between these two approaches by looking at a specific passage of Scripture. A little later in the Song of Songs we find the following passage:

The voice of my beloved!
　Look, he comes,
leaping upon the mountains,
　bounding over the hills.
My beloved is like a gazelle
　or a young stag.
Look, there he stands
　behind our wall,
gazing in at the windows,
　looking through the lattice.
My beloved speaks and says to me:
"Arise, my love, my fair one,
　and come away." (Song 2:8-10)

If we come to this text as theorists, we find we have many lines of approach. We might begin by examining the text as a whole. Although Jewish and Christian piety has traditionally taken this song as an exchange between God and his people, the lack of any direct reference to God together with the frankly erotic imagery used throughout might suggest to us that it was probably composed simply as a series of poems expressing love between a man and woman. Was Solomon that man? Although the poem calls itself "the Song of Songs, which is Solomon's" (Song 1:1), it is not clear what that implies—whether it was written by Solomon or for Solomon or just in the style of Solomon. At any rate, it seems unlikely that this great king would have been wandering around the hill country peering into latticed windows in the hope of catching sight of an agricultural laboring girl. Perhaps, then, we should conclude that this exchange of verse takes place between an anonymous Hebrew couple, some few centuries before Christ.

With that knowledge in hand, we can begin to look at this specific passage. There is a picturesque image in a few lines which could catch our attention, comparing the young man to a gazelle and a stag. Is there more to these words than meet the eye? Some scholars have noted that, a few lines before, the young woman uses the curious phrase "by the gazelles or the wild does" (Song 2:7). The words are phrased like an oath, but an oath that avoids using the divine name—as though the poet were seeking to allude to God without actually mentioning him, a dramatic device to show respect for the divine in an essentially secular piece. Interestingly, Shakespeare frequently has his characters draw on mythological gods and heroes for the same reason, to avoid mentioning God directly. Others have observed that gazelles and deer were themselves divine symbols, emblems of the Canaanite goddess of love. So comparing the man to a gazelle or a stag might be a way of suggesting he is some kind of "love god"—rather like calling a man an "Adonis" today.

Is this knowledge interesting and illuminating? Of course. Does it take us a little further and deeper into the world of the text and enhance our understanding? Undoubtedly. This is the gift good scholarship offers us.

But where does it end? We could continue analyzing these words almost indefinitely. We could make comparisons with other ancient Near Eastern poetry. We could examine the tradition of translation into Greek, Latin, Coptic, Syriac, English. Countless other areas of study begin to open up: ancient courting customs, Hebrew architecture (to better understand "looking through the lattice"), textual variations, the interpretation of the Song through the ages, the use of the text in Jewish and Christian liturgies—the list goes on. And if we only ask these questions and never move beyond them, we will be excellent theorists, but nothing more.

My Beloved Speaks—to Me

The lover finds this study and knowledge interesting. Helpful. Essential, even. But for the lover, merely studying this text would be to miss the point entirely. It may well be that this passage was originally written simply as a poem celebrating human love, with no theological dimension intended. No matter. Here, in Scripture, it can speak equally well of our yearning for the divine lover and his desire for us. This is not only the "Song of Songs which is Solomon's," it is also the song of the soul, our song. As we open the Bible and open ourselves to the presence of God in Scripture, we echo the words of the young woman: "The voice of my beloved! Look, he comes!" Truly our Lover, too, is like the gazelle and stag, for he is the God of love. And in the words of the Song we hear his voice: "Arise, my love, my fair one, and come away." These words are addressed to us: to the church, to God's people, to the soul, to the heart—to me.

The twelfth-century abbot Bernard of Clairvaux knew how to read Scripture as a lover. In his monumental series of sermons on the Song of Songs, he read this same passage in the light of his own passionate longing for intimacy with God. As he considered the image of the young man peering through the latticed window, seeking a glimpse of his beloved, Bernard saw a parallel in his relationship with Christ. "He also stands behind the wall," he wrote,

> as long as this body of ours, which is certainly sinful, hides his face from us and shuts out his presence. For "so long as we are in this body we are exiles of the Lord" (2 Corinthians 5:6)—not because we are embodied . . . it is not our bodies but our sins that stand in the way. . . . How close he is to the bride who is separated by one wall only! On this account she longs that the dividing wall be broken down.

And so for Bernard this is no mere love poem: it cannot be read simply as an account of a torrid affair between an anonymous Near Eastern couple, now many centuries dead. Bernard is saying: Here I discover a reflection of my life in Christ. And here, listening as a lover, I hear the voice of my Beloved.

> He says, "Arise, make haste, my love, my dove, my beautiful one." Happy the conscience which deserves to hear those words! Who among us, do you think, is so vigilant, so attentive to the time of his visitation and the Bridegroom's coming that he every moment scans every detail of his approach, so that when [the Bridegroom] comes and knocks, he opens the door to him right away?

For Bernard, the words of the Song are not only contemporary and relevant, they are the words of Christ himself, speaking in the present straight into the life and heart of the reader. The Bible, here at least, does not merely inform faith in God, it mediates an encounter with God.

But is the lover's reading limited to the more obviously passionate and affective parts of Scripture, like Song of Songs or Psalms? Not at all. The living presence of God runs through the whole of the Bible, a constant thread from start to finish, and a lover is able to be attentive to that presence everywhere—in the laws as much as the lauds, in dry theology as much as fiery theophany.

A theorist approaches Romans. Paul's grand narrative of salvation is carefully dismantled so that every piece can be examined and analyzed. Subtle nuances are noted; overarching themes are headlined. Finally, the pieces are reconstructed into a framework rather more systematic, more thorough—in fact, the theology we feel Paul himself might have written if he had enjoyed the luxury of working in a university library rather than in the confines of a prison cell. But lovers experience the estrangement from God Paul describes, and the bitter taste of sin in the mouth. And so they read through tears, weeping with Paul: "Wretched man that I am! Who will rescue me from this body of death?" They echo his shout of wonder in the face of grace: "Thanks be to God through Jesus Christ our Lord!" (Rom 7:24-25). Lovers linger in Romans because here they can soak in grace—even when they cannot define it.

The theorist comes to Leviticus to determine the book's authorship and origin, to establish when the book was written, to explore the role of the priesthood in ancient Israel, to reconstruct cultic life in the Jerusalem temple, to elucidate the differences between holy and unholy, clean and unclean. The lover comes to learn what it means to be presented as a "living sacrifice, holy and acceptable to God" (Rom 12:1)—how to express a prayer of longing that goes beyond words, that absorbs our possessions, our livelihood, our very selves. Theorists explain the offerings, but lovers become one.

Both approaches are possible. But in the end the Bible was not written for theorists. It is the book of lovers.

Readings

No book of Scripture expresses more passionately nor more profoundly the love between God and his people than the Song of Songs. If we want to learn to orient our hearts more fully toward him as we read the Bible, spending time praying through this short book will prove an invaluable investment.

As you approach these passages, I advise you to do little more than allow them to sweep you up and carry you along in the intensity of their love. For now, set aside analysis and dissection. Hear the words of the Lover as God's words to you, to your soul. Turn the responses of the Beloved into prayer, your response to God. Try to resist the temptation to tone down the intensity of this poem. Let this book stimulate you to desire God with all your being.

Day 1	Song of Songs 1:1-8	(Let him kiss me!)
Day 2	Song of Songs 1:9-17	(you are beautiful, my love)
Day 3	Song of Songs 2:1-7	(his fruit was sweet)
Day 4	Song of Songs 2:8-17	(My beloved speaks)

Day 5   Song of Songs 3:1-5   (I sought him)
Day 6   Song of Songs 3:6-11   (inlaid with love)
Day 7   Song of Songs 4:1-8   (How beautiful you are!)

6

READING LIKE LOVERS

When my wife and I were courting ("dating" if you like, although we preferred the elegant overtones of the more old-fashioned word), we lived at opposite ends of the British Isles. I was in my final year of study at Aberystwyth University, on the west Wales coast, and she was finishing her masters degree at Dundee, way up on the east coast of Scotland. In those distant days before the advent of cell phones and e-mail, and with little money available to afford travel, we relied a great deal on the Royal Mail to keep our relationship alive.

A few days ago I went down into the basement, opened one of the ragged cardboard boxes we use for storage, and pulled out two battered and scratched biscuit tins. Inside were all the letters Sally sent me during the year or so we lived apart—we wrote to one another almost every day, so the letters number in the hundreds. They are bundled together in fairly random order, and each one represents only her half of our long-distance correspondence. It's hard now to piece together the lines of conversation. After more than twenty years, I have trouble putting faces to some of the names. The news she shares about friends is like some garbled code, depending on my understanding of jokes or incidents long forgotten. Occasionally small items fall out of the envelope—a lock of hair, when she had her long ponytail trimmed off, a picture postcard, some clipping from a newspaper. It's an odd experience reading these letters now, as though I were an archaeologist unearthing the earliest layers of our friendship and finding them far more mysterious than I expected.

I suppose if I had enough time I could order them by dates, tease out the storylines, track down the details of individuals, catalogue the odd enclosures, piece together the whole story again. It might be fun. Perhaps, one day, my future grandchildren might do just that. To them, the mystery of their ancestor's lives might present a challenging puzzle, a fascinating riddle of family history to be unraveled on rainy evenings. But I have more pleasure just holding the letters and remembering what they represent. They call up memories and emotions from which my marriage grew and flourished. I enjoy reading these letters, but not analyzing them. They remind me of the length and depth of our love for one another, the ever-lengthening story we have woven together.

I'm content to let others come and be theorists with these letters. I read them as a lover. It would be impossible to come to them any other way.

Prayerful and Empty

How can we learn to come to the Bible in this way, as lovers and not simply theorists? As we come to Scripture, there are at least four attitudes we can choose to adopt which will help draw us more deeply into the presence of God as we read.

First, we can choose to read prayerfully. In my home we always say grace before every meal. In fact, we usually sing grace together, often quite loudly and enthusiastically! This practice has helped us to recognize the presence of God among us as we eat, and to come to the table with a great deal more gratitude, even for those meals that have turned out to be less gourmet delight and more burned offering (usually the dishes I have cooked). It is possible to practice the same discipline with Scripture. I have worshiped in churches where the readers always pray before opening the Bible; in some liturgical churches there is an elaborate ritual of blessings, prayers, processions and incense waving before a single word is read. This helps the congregation to be attentive—not only to the words being read but to God present in those words.

We can choose, as individuals, to adopt a similar discipline, developing the habit of turning our hearts toward God every single time we pick up the Bible. The Bible itself provides a number of marvelous prayers we might use. For example:

> Let me see your face,
>   let me hear your voice;
> for your voice is sweet,
>   and your face is lovely. (Song 2:14)

> Open my eyes, so that I may behold
>   wondrous things out of your law. (Ps 119:18)

> Speak, LORD, for your servant is listening. (1 Sam 3:9)

Learning to begin in this way is a first step toward prayerful reading, but not the whole story. It is also important to remain in an attitude of prayer as we continue to read, keeping ourselves oriented toward God speaking to us through the Bible, rather than allowing ourselves to get caught up in our own thoughts, concerns and clever reflections. When I'm reading the Bible, I usually have a pencil in hand to underline passages that strike me for any reason (sometimes they seem particularly important, or they puzzle me, or perhaps I simply enjoy the way they are worded). I find it a helpful practice to pause every time I scratch my pencil across the page, and look for a way to allow that striking moment to become a prayerful moment. This ensures that my study and learning develop into conversation and open listening. Over time, those underlinings are becoming a shorthand journal of my journey with God.

Second, we can choose to read with empty hands. It is always tempting to come to the Bible with an agenda. We might read to confirm our theological system or to find arguments to challenge someone else's ideas. Perhaps we read to find guidance for life, to seek answers to our big questions, to solve our pressing dilemmas. Certainly many of us will have favorite stories, poems, verses or sayings we turn to again and again, usually because we are confident before we read that we know what they will say to us. None of this is necessarily wrong—but all these ways of reading place us in control and blunt the capacity of the Bible to shock us, to surprise us, to derail us. The problem is, of course, that our agenda may not be God's agenda.

To read with empty hands means setting aside our agenda and developing an interior silence. To paraphrase the prayer quoted earlier, it means that rather than saying, "Speak, Lord—about this pressing matter," we will pray, "Speak, Lord—about whatever you desire—for your servant is listening." Without this silence we may technically be reading the Word of God in Scripture, but since we are trying to determine in advance what that Word will say, it is much harder for us to hear the living voice of God speaking through that Word.

This is one of the reasons Christians through the ages have always recommended a varied diet of reading that ranges across the whole of Scripture. Churches will often follow lectionaries or work through different books of the Bible in course. Individuals might use a daily reading plan or a Bible divided into dated passages for every day. I am far too disorganized to follow a reading plan properly; I often mislay the reading scheme or get confused when I miss a day. So I simply work my way through different books of

the Bible, writing the date alongside a passage whenever I begin to
read, and marking the margin wherever I finish so I know where
to pick up next time. After a while, it becomes clear which books
I have not read in a while. I also begin to notice which passages
keep drawing my attention; that helps me understand my own
agenda more clearly, and so I become a little more able to set it
aside and come to Scripture with empty hands.

Humble and Expectant

Third, we can choose to read in humility, which means reading
with a readiness to be obedient. We can find it difficult to understand the relationship between obedience and love, since in our
society they often seem to be diametric opposites. Since the Ro-
mantic movement in the eighteenth century, our culture has
tended to define love in terms of emotion: it is the feelings I have
within myself that signal the possibility that this person is my
potential soul mate, that form the basis for a developing intimacy,
that, in the end, will bind me to my lover. And, of course, should
those feelings wane at any point (as they inevitably will), this can
be taken as a sign that love has died, that the relationship is over
and it is time for me to move on. Obedience and submission seem
to be the very antithesis of love defined in this way: they imply a
commitment to continue to live and walk together regardless of
the state of my feelings, and to accept a relationship in which my
fulfillment, joy and pleasure are not paramount.

This, though, is precisely how love is defined in Scripture.
The words of the Shema, found in Deuteronomy 6:4-5, are still
recited daily by devout Jews, and were quoted by Jesus as part of
his summation of the law: "Hear, O Israel: The LORD is our God,
the LORD alone. You shall love the LORD your God with all your
heart, and with all your soul, and with all your might." But what
exactly is the nature of that love? Is it the feelings God stirs up
within us, a reaching out to him of our bubbling emotions? Not

according to the verses that surround the statement. "Fear the LORD your God all the days of your life," says Moses immediately before reciting the Shema, "and keep all his decrees and his commandments that I am commanding you" (v. 2). In the same spirit he follows the great call to love by reminding the Hebrews to "keep these words I am commanding you today in your heart"— which was less a recommendation that they be memorized, and more a summons to incarnate them from the innermost part of our being. Love is committed and responsive: "If you love me," said Jesus, "you will keep my commandments" (Jn 14:15). The true lover of God is not the one who comes to Scripture looking for an inspirational rush, but the one who comes ready to listen attentively and act accordingly.

Paradoxically, however, reading obediently does not always mean simply doing whatever the text tells us to do. When Jesus says to "pray for those who persecute you" (Mt 5:44), there is little doubt that this is exactly what he expects us to do: the obedient heart will seek to respond appropriately. On the other hand, Jesus also says to the rich young ruler: "Sell all that you own and distribute the money to the poor, and you will have treasure in heaven; then come, follow me" (Lk 18:22). As we saw in chapter one, that call struck both Antony of Egypt and Francis of Assisi very directly, and they responded with wholehearted and literal obedience. But there are good reasons for thinking that this is not Jesus' call to each person who seeks to follow him faithfully; even his original disciples were not all called to such radical self-renunciation. So a humble and obedient reading of this call requires not only listening to the words themselves but also being attentive to the voice of the Spirit present in the words; the Spirit helps us discern how we should live in response to Scripture, as Jesus said: "the Holy Spirit, whom the Father will send in my name, will teach you everything" (Jn 14:26).

Last, we can choose to read expectantly. When Moses approached the burning bush, he said to himself, "I must turn aside and look at this great sight, and see why the bush is not burned up" (Ex 3:3). He knew he was coming into the presence of something extraordinary—even though he had no idea exactly what it was. His mind and heart were open. This is the perfect way to begin reading the Bible.

The Bible itself recounts a tremendous example of such an open-hearted reading of Scripture. After the dramatic events of Belshazzar's feast—when the ghostly hand wrote its message of doom on the wall and the Babylonian kingdom fell into the hands of the Persians—Daniel found himself absorbed in reading from the prophetic books of Scripture. "I, Daniel, perceived in the books the number of years that, according to the word of the LORD to the prophet Jeremiah, must be fulfilled for the devastation of Jerusalem, namely, seventy years" (Dan 9:2). At this moment Daniel may well have faced the temptation to read as a theorist, as countless others have done since. He could have carefully compared historical accounts and calculated dates, allowing him to predict the exact time of Jerusalem's restoration. He might then have been able to locate this within a wider framework of Israelite chronology, past and future, integrating the message of the prophets into a sweeping theological history from earthly creation to heavenly consummation. Then Daniel could have presented himself as one who had mastered the interpretation of God's intentions in history: one who knows the future.

Instead, Daniel allows his heart to be struck. He surveyed the scale of the catastrophe outlined by Jeremiah: the downfall of Judah, the sacking of the temple and seventy years of exile in a godless land. And all this because of the people's betrayal of their covenant relationship with God. Overwhelmed, Daniel falls to his knees in contrition. "Ah Lord, great and awesome God," he prays with tears, "we have sinned and done wrong, acted wickedly and rebelled. . . . Righteousness is on your side, O Lord, but open shame, as at this day, falls on us, the people of Judah. . . . O Lord, hear; O Lord, forgive; O Lord, listen and act and do not delay!" (see Dan 9:4-19 for the whole prayer). And then, unexpectedly, Daniel receives a response—an angelic visitation. "While I was speaking in prayer, the man Gabriel, whom I had seen before in a vision, came to me in swift flight at the time of the evening sacrifice" (Dan 9:21).

Daniel came to Scripture expectantly, and so his reading led naturally to prayer, and from prayer to an experience of divine presence. It is possible for us to come to the Bible in the same spirit: not looking for brilliant insights, new knowledge or confirmation of our already entrenched opinions, but seeking instead the Author's presence and fully anticipating that he will come to meet us.

Here, then, is our starting point for a fresh reading of Scripture. Not resisting the insights of the scholars, but at the same time refusing to read merely as theorists. Not denying the liberal conviction that the Bible presents us with a window into the past, an opportunity to share the inspiring experiences of previous generations; nor denying the conservative conviction that Scripture can be a nourishing well of propositions, a deep spring of eternal truth with timeless relevance. But determined to push beyond this, to read as lovers, to approach the Bible as an opportunity for encounter, as the medium of the divine kiss, as a way into presence.

Readings

As we continue reading through the Song of Songs, come to each of these texts in the way described in this chapter. This is a particularly easy text to read as a lover; practicing with these passages will prepare your heart to approach some of the more challenging passages of Scripture (like Leviticus!).

Prepare yourself to read prayerfully, open to the presence of

God being made known through this poetry. Come with empty
hands, with a willingness to let God set the pace. Be humble and
alert to his calling on your life. And, of course, be expectant—
as you read, God is with you. Who knows where this reading
might lead?

Day 1   Song of Songs 4:9–5:1   (You have ravished my heart)
Day 2   Song of Songs 5:2-8   (I am faint with love)
Day 3   Song of Songs 5:9–6:3   (This is my beloved)
Day 4   Song of Songs 6:4-13   (Turn away your eyes)
Day 5   Song of Songs 7:1-9   (How fair and pleasant you are!)
Day 6   Song of Songs 7:10–8:4   (I am my beloved's)
Day 7   Song of Songs 8:5-14   (love is strong as death)

7

ANATOMY OF THE SOUL

Setting fire to a tub full of kerosene seemed like a great idea at the time. We were twelve years old, filled with the naiveté of youth and didn't know any better. With the benefit of hindsight I realize it may have been more than a little foolish.

We were enjoying one of those gloriously endless summer afternoons that were apparently so abundant a few decades ago. Now, in my adult life, I discover that they have been made fleeting and filled with an awareness of lawns that need mowing and fences that could use a coat of paint. But then we had eternity at our fingertips and a world of wonders to unearth. Kevin and I had spent a productive morning over at the golf course: hidden in thick undergrowth between a couple of winding fairways we were ideally placed to sprint out from time to time into the rough grass or a nearby sand trap and steal recently arrived golf balls, then race back to cover and watch the puzzled search that followed. Later we wandered back to the nineteenth hole and sold the loot we had so helpfully "found" for a tidy profit, before retreating under a nearby bridge to half choke ourselves to death on an improvised homemade cigarette.

And somewhere in that afternoon we found ourselves in the long garden behind Kevin's house contemplating a delightfully unguarded barrel of kerosene nestled among his father's shovels and rakes in the damp and rickety shed. What common sense we had was blinded, overcome, by the simple universal truth hard-wired into our genetic code: men want to make fire. And we boys so wanted to be men. Clearly, here before us was two dozen gallons of liquid rite of passage.

Kevin rooted through the junk on the musty shelves and produced a large plastic margarine tub and a cobwebbed box of safety matches. Unscrewing the rusty cap on the barrel, we leaned it forward and filled the tub with kerosene to within half an inch of the top. I carried the tub out into the garden, careful not to spill a drop of this magical fluid, and gently put it down in the very center of the lawn. Kevin followed with the matches. Protocol demanded that Kevin be the maker of fire; this was, after all, his father's garden and his father's fuel.

Kevin knelt before the tub, struck a match, and gingerly reached out his hand to touch the flame to the liquid.

I confess the result was initially disappointing. Although Kevin was a good friend, I had naturally hoped that the kerosene would explode violently and noisily, perhaps lifting Kevin from the ground and tossing him across the garden like a rag doll. After all, that's what would happen in a movie. Instead there was a quiet puffing sound as flames licked across the surface of the liquid, followed by a few seconds of guttering fire. We stood back to watch, pensive and underwhelmed.

And then I noticed the lip of the tub beginning to curl outward as the heat of the flames melted the thin plastic. We watched in appalled fascination as the edges began to soften, as tiny grooves sank down to become deep valleys. The burning kerosene began to trickle through, dripping onto the grass around the tub. Then, very suddenly, the edges gave way and a lake of fire rolled toward us.

It's incredible how much liquid a single margarine tub can hold. As we scrambled back toward the house a huge flaming circle radiated out across Kevin's lawn. Time slowed. We watched in horror as every blade of grass became a tiny wick for this roiling, unstoppable flood of fire. Had we read Dante's *Inferno*, we might perhaps have realized that we were standing on the edge of one of the deeper circles of hell: the burning sea reserved for the insatiably mischievous. Even without Dante's help we knew we were shortly destined for the afterlife; if the fire didn't kill us, Kevin's father surely would. The circle had enveloped most of the lawn, and surely would spread to the fences, the houses around, across the street—in a moment of panic we realized we may have set the flame that would consume the world.

Those few seconds stretched themselves to the breaking point. And then, suddenly, time snapped back to its normal pace. The kerosene burned out, and with a few whispering pops the fire evaporated. Kevin and I stood looking out over a strangely transformed lawn. The formerly lush green grass was now an odd patchwork of greasy yellows and browns; in the center lay a surreal sculpture of twisted white plastic fused to the scorched earth. It had a peculiar, ethereal appeal (at least to us), but by no reach of the imagination could it ever be called beautiful. It was not, I realized, the lawn Kevin's father would want to come home to.

And come home he would—soon. I looked Kevin in the eye. His face was imploring. Stay with me, it seemed to say. We are men! Together we have made fire! Now together let us face the oncoming wrath!

"Bye, Kevin!" I yelled as I ran like the wind for the safety of home.

Participants, Not Observers

I learned an invaluable lesson that summer afternoon (although I didn't know it at the time): there are no disinterested observers in the universe, only engaged participants.

Years later, while studying quantum mechanics at Aberystwyth University, I encountered the same idea in a rather more rarified form known as the Heisenberg Uncertainty Principle. In 1927 the German physicist Werner Heisenberg demonstrated that it is not possible to measure accurately all the properties of a single subatomic particle because the action of making measurements causes unpredictable changes in the very system being measured. In order to make any kind of measurement, an observer has to add some kind of energy somewhere—for example, if we want to use a ruler to measure the length of a piece of wood, we need to shine enough light on the ruler to be able to read the scale. We don't normally notice the effect of such a simple action, but at the incredibly tiny scale of atomic physics even miniscule infusions of energy cause dramatic effects. So the energy used to measure the location and speed of a moving electron causes it to change course, which means we can only determine the speed and location it had before we touched it.

Until Heisenberg's discovery one of the fundamental assumptions of science was that good researchers would always be objective, uninvolved, standing outside the systems they sought to study. It was almost as though the entire universe were sealed in a sterile bubble while the scientist somehow stood on the outside— looking in, observing, making notes, learning, but never interacting. Any involvement of the researcher in the system might invalidate the results of the experiment.

But the Uncertainty Principle, although it essentially applied only to the very limited field of quantum physics, blew a hole right through this assumption. The effects of this simple discovery are still being felt across the natural sciences to the present day. Heisenberg had demonstrated that, in the end, pure objectivity is impossible. We are involved in the universe, intricately bound into the whole system, and our every act affects both us and the universe around us—even the act of trying to study the universe disinterestedly and objectively. We cannot help being engaged. We are never silent watchers on the sidelines, but always participants, whether we like it or not.

The same is true of our reading of Scripture. The Bible is a vast, intricate and magnificent spiritual universe of stories, ideas, songs, poetry, wisdom and prophecy, within which we can walk and dwell with God. But this is not a universe we visit from a distance, peering in from afar like astronomers searching the distant reaches of the galaxy. We are participants in this spiritual world. The story of Scripture is *our* story, the story of God shaping our world and our lives; the songs of the Bible echo the song of our souls. Scriptural prophecy reaches into our present and future.

Inescapably, we bring ourselves into our reading. The act of engaging with Scripture changes us, and readers who share their readings change each other. Every act of reading transforms both the readers and the reading community they belong to. Scripture has no objective observers. We are involved. We are participants.

In order to understand the process of reading Scripture, then, we need a clear picture not only of the character of the Bible but also of the nature of the reader of Scripture: ourselves. Just as it is important to understand how the different types of biblical writing weave together to form a coherent whole—how history interacts with prophecy, and wisdom with epistolary writing—in order to develop a sense of the overall message of the Bible, so also we need to understand how the different aspects of the human person are involved in the act of reading, and how Scripture affects each one. We need to clarify the anatomy of the reader. But the anatomy we need to study is not that outlined by physicians and biologists; the location and function of the spleen or liver won't give us much insight into our engagement with the Bible. We need to understand ourselves as both physical and spiritual beings—to have an integrated view of our mind, our emotions, our will. We need not only an anatomy of the body but also an anatomy of the soul.

A Map of the Soul

This figure sketches out the relationship between various aspects of our inner person—a sketch map of the reader's soul, if you like.

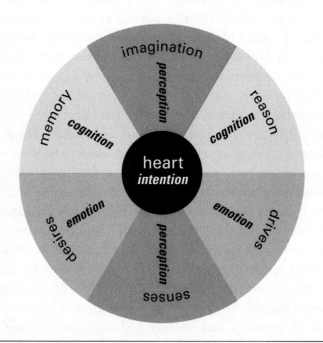

The interactions of seven aspects of the inner life

Seven different aspects of the inner life interact with one another to enable some of the most important activities of the soul. Our senses and imagination together create the possibility of *perception*, the ability to experience the world around us and form an intelligent and coherent picture of it. A variety of desires and drives combine to create our *emotions*, the tools to react appropriately to the world we experience (for example, by desiring healthy food rather than poisonous fungi, or by reacting with courageous drive when our loved ones are in danger). Memory and reason allow *cognition* or thought, the process of reflecting on past and current experiences in order to discover order and meaning in our lives and our world, and to predict the consequences of events and actions.

Finally the heart is able to take all of these elements—our perceptions, emotions and cognition—and create intention. The original Latin word *intendere* implied one thing "stretching into" another. Some of our intentions are acts of the will shaping deliberate actions and habits of life; through these we "stretch" into the future. Others are acts of the spirit, when we form relationships with God and other people around us, "stretching" into the life of another. The medieval French writer Jean Gerson once defined prayer as *animi extensio in Deum per amoris desiderium:* the soul stretching into God through loving desire. This is the work of the heart, orienting us outward to love—although, of course, our fallen hearts rather too often find themselves orienting inward and sinking into destructive self-absorption.

Where did this picture of our inner anatomy come from? In large part the diagram draws on the classical Christian understanding of the inner life, developed over the centuries from the foundations laid by the writers of Scripture. Since neither the Hebrew Bible nor the New Testament writings contain any systematic analysis of the faculties of the inner self, this traditional Christian understanding of human nature was created by incorporating the scattered clues found throughout Scripture into the prevailing intellectual models developed by the great Greek philosophers and the medieval theological tradition. Three writers in particular played critical roles in shaping this Christian view of the soul: Plato, Aristotle and (of course) the apostle Paul.

The Chariot

Plato, in the *Phaedrus* (a dialogue written around the same time as the more famous *Republic*) uses a compelling image to describe his view of human nature. Imagine a flying chariot being drawn through the sky by a pair of winged horses, each with a very different character. On one side of the pair, as Plato describes it, is a noble white horse, disciplined and strong, which seeks to pull the chariot heavenward; on the other is a horse dark and wild, unpredictably dangerous and longing to drag the chariot down to earth. These two horses, Plato tells us, represent two sets of conflicting impulses or emotions. The noble horse symbolizes our *drives*, our forceful courage and determination—the kind of spiritedness that might succeed in drawing us beyond our own limitations and into a richer experience of reality. But this is constantly at war with another powerful impulse within us, an inner force represented by the dark horse: our base appetites and *desires*. These, Plato argued, are constantly seeking to lure us back down to the grime of earth, to corrupt and demean us by smothering our divine nature with the banalities of the material world. (Plato, of course, was heir to a Greek philosophical tradition that accepted a much sharper opposition between the spiritual and material world, between soul and body, than we see in the biblical worldview.)

As these two horses drive the chariot forward in two conflicting directions, it becomes the responsibility of the charioteer to control and maneuver them so that their energy can be harnessed, rather than allowing it to tear the whole arrangement apart. This charioteer of the human soul, Plato wrote, is *reason*: the thinking faculty within the human soul that is able to discern how the forces exerted by conflicting human emotions will affect the whole person. Usually reason will seek to allow the nobler emotions—the courageous and determined human spirit—to prevail over the baser passions, but at times it will be necessary to allow the appetites and desires greater freedom to prevent the whole person from becoming unbalanced. Neither horse is capable of moderating the other in Plato's allegory; only reason, with a firm grasp on the reins, is able to hold a steady course. (Readers of the *Republic*, where Plato developed these ideas in some detail, will readily recognize this threefold picture of the soul.)

An Image of the World

Plato's student and successor, Aristotle, accepted some aspects of this picture, changed a few and rejected yet others. But his main contribution to the Christian tradition came through his study of aspects of the soul Plato had overlooked.

First, Aristotle paid far more attention to the question of perception: How does the human soul experience and interpret the material world? Aristotle's first step in analyzing this was to identify the familiar five physical *senses*: sight, hearing, touch, smell and taste. Each of these senses enables us to receive information about the world around us. But how does the mind integrate the very different sensations presented to it into a single, coherent mental representation?

Think of eating a slice of lemon, for example. As you bite into it your mind is battered by a volley of sensory experiences. You see the bright yellow half-moon slice. Your fingers touch the thick, rough rind and feel the wet, sticky juice. You smell the sharply refreshing lemon odor. And your tongue is shocked by the fruit's tart sourness. But in your mind all these sensations blend together into one single idea: the lemon itself.

Aristotle suggested that the senses are integrated by the *imagination*, the aspect of the soul that creates an inner image of realities in the external world. Once this inner representation is created it can be manipulated by the mind and combined with other similar (or dissimilar) images to create new ideas, perspectives and views of reality. Through our cumulative experience of actual reality, we gather the mental tools not only to imagine what is materially present to us through our senses but also to imagine the merely *possible*. Having seen a red flower and a gray elephant, for example, I find myself easily able to imagine a red elephant, even though I've never seen or heard of such a beast. Art feeds on this faculty of imagination; almost all forms of artistic endeavor depend on this ability to conceive of and somehow express possible realities that we have not experienced.

Then Aristotle began the explore the subject of *memory* (he devoted an entire short treatise to the subject of memory and recollection). He saw our memories as a kind of repository of all the integrated images produced by our imagination's acts of perception; a storehouse of experiences available to the rational mind. By drawing on the memory our reason is able to fashion a framework for understanding the world around us. By studying past experience it can begin to predict the way future experiences will unfold. If I have hurt my hand every time it has been closely exposed to flames, my reasoning mind can safely deduce that putting my hand into *this* fire will also be painful.

This leads to a threefold picture of the mind (or soul—the same Greek word, *psychē*, is used for both concepts). Our physical senses receive all kinds of strange and wonderful sensations from the universe around us. The imagination integrates this sensory input, allowing us to experience the present, the world immediately around us. Over time the images created by the imagination form our memory, allowing us to re-experience the *past*; our memory is the story which sets our trajectories, variously warning, encouraging and comforting us in the present. Our capacity to reason allows us to manipulate images both from our memory and from our immediate perceptions of the present and combine them to understand more fully the world in which we live—and, of course, to make reliable predictions about the *future*.

Paul's Perspective

These six different aspects of the inner life—drives, desires, reason, senses, imagination and memory—became crucial elements of the Christian understanding of the human person. With a framework somewhat along these lines in their minds, our ancestors in the faith—from the writers of the New Testament onward—approached Scripture to explore the nature of the soul. The model with which they emerged from that study of the Bible retained all these elements but, crucially, saw them all in an entirely fresh light.

Of all the New Testament writers Paul offered the richest and deepest thinking on the nature of the human person. But Paul was not a systematic writer, even though texts like Romans might initially seem to suggest otherwise. The only writings of Paul that have survived are in the form of either open letters to communities or more personal letters to individuals, almost always written in response to specific crises and questions. These epistles were composed during his extensive travels around the eastern Roman empire, often from the discomfort of a prison cell. These were not conditions conducive to producing an academic thesis on systematic theology. Reading his letters, though, is like peering through scattered openings into an extraordinarily fertile mind; while we cannot always arrange his ideas into neat rows and columns, we will always find ourselves stimulated and challenged to think afresh. This is especially the case when we consider Paul's perspective on the human soul.

Paul's theology is worked out in the tension between two opposing realities about humanity: we are created in the image and likeness of God, and called "good" (Gen 1:26-27, 31), but we are utterly fallen and corrupted by sin (Rom 3:10-18). Because of the latter, Paul cannot be as sanguine as Plato about the ability of both reason and our noble "spiritedness" to keep in check our base desires. He understands that our desires and appetites are natural and appropriate in themselves (there is no sin in feeling a desire for food or water!), but that they have been warped and twisted by sin into something far more destructive: "fornication, impurity, licentiousness, . . . drunkenness, carousing, and things like these" (Gal 5:19-21). But in the same passage in Galatians, Paul also notes that our forceful drives, which Plato symbolized as a majestic white stallion, have been equally tainted by sin; he warns his readers against "enmities, strife, jealousy, anger, dissensions, factions, envy."

What of reason, the charioteer who is expected to guide these wayward beasts? Unfortunately, says Paul, our mind has also become depraved, has lost its bearings; hence the need to "destroy arguments and every proud obstacle raised up against the knowledge of God, and . . . take every thought captive to obey Christ" (2 Cor 10:4-5).

We can easily extend Paul's line of thought to include Aristotle's additions to this model: our perception is skewed (both senses and imagination) and our memory distorted. Every aspect of the soul, although made good by God, has been dragged down and soiled by sin.

Paul also injects an extra dimension of human experience into the mixture. He distinguishes, as any Greek might have done, between the body (*sōma*)—the expression of a human being in the material world—and the soul or mind (*psychē*), the inner life of that person. But he also distinguishes carefully within that inner life between the soul and the "spirit" (*pneuma*). In 1 Thessalonians 5:23 Paul writes: "May the God of peace himself sanctify you entirely; and may your spirit [*pneuma*] and soul [*psychē*] and body [*sōma*] be kept sound and blameless at the coming of our Lord Jesus Christ." A similar distinction is made by the author of the letter to the Hebrews (traditionally identified as Paul, but now regarded by most scholars as from a separate, anonymous hand): "the word of God is living and active, sharper than any two-edged

sword, piercing until it divides soul [*psychē*] from spirit [*pneuma*]"
(Heb 4:12).

Paul never formally defines the distinction between spirit and
soul. But it is clear from his letters that, like other Greek writers,
he very closely aligns the soul with the mind; it is in this part of
our inner world that we are able to construct ideas, combine them
with other ideas we have formed in the past, and make deductions
about the universe around us. The soul, or mind, is where imagination, memory and reason combine. The spirit, though, seems to
be something more—although Paul doesn't state precisely what
that something more might be. It clearly is related to our being
made in the image and likeness of God, since God is essentially
spirit. It is also what allows us most fully to know ourselves and
know God, as Paul tells the Corinthians:

> For what human being knows what is truly human except
> the human spirit that is within? So also no one comprehends
> what is truly God's except the Spirit of God. Now we have
> received not the spirit of the world, but the Spirit that is from
> God, so that we may understand the gifts bestowed on us by
> God. And we speak of these things in words not taught by
> human wisdom but taught by the Spirit, interpreting spiri-
> tual things to those who are spiritual. (1 Cor 2:11-13)

Paul also draws a close connection between the spirit (*pneuma*),
the will (*thelēma*), and the heart (*kardia*). We tend to think of the
heart as the seat of emotion and passion—influenced by the lin-
gering legacy of eighteenth- and nineteenth-century Romanticism,
which sought to place emotions and feeling at the very center of
human experience. But for Paul, our emotions, our desires and
drives are hardwired into our bodies as a whole (see, for example,
Rom 7:5); they are not the center of our personality but means by
which we express that personality. For Paul, the heart is the seat
of the *will*; it is in the heart that we form our intentions and pur-

poses (1 Cor 4:5). But it is also in the heart that the Spirit of God most closely dwells with us (2 Cor 1:22). These three—heart, will and spirit—seem intimately bound together in Paul's thought.

Becoming Fully Present

Here we are then: creatures of two worlds, of the physical and spiritual universes, blended into a single person. We are physical beings, made of cells, bones, blood and organs. We can sense the material world, move in it, interact with it. But we are also spiritual beings; we perceive the inner world too, move freely within it, relate to it and affect it. And these two are intimately bound together. Our emotions, memories, reason, even our will can be shaped by diet, injury or illness. Conversely, our state of mind, our will, our prayer seem to be able to mold our health and physical well-being. We are bodies and souls—and spirits too, fashioned to extend our lives into one another and finally into God.

The pressing question is: how can we bring the entirety of our being to the reading of Scripture? As we learn to approach the Bible as lovers rather than as theorists, we discover the startling degree to which God reveals himself, makes himself known, manifests himself to us through the act of reading. God is fully present to us as we meet him on the holy ground of Scripture.

We, on the other hand, are often rather less fully present to God. In the contemporary Western church we have a strong tendency to read the Bible as a largely intellectual exercise. We examine, analyze, categorize, systematize. Our minds—especially our ability to reason—are fully engaged. But how do we bring the rest of our selves into the presence of God through reading? How can we involve our senses and imagination? Our emotions, those desires and drives that pulse through us so strongly? Our memory? And, most of all, our heart—that fount of intention which so longs to stretch into God through loving desire?

We cannot come to the Bible as disinterested observers. How

then can we throw ourselves into its world as eager participants? The remainder of this book explores a variety of ways in which Christians throughout the ages have sought to read Scripture as a means to encounter God. These different approaches tend to emphasize one or another of these aspects of the soul. First we consider our *perception* of the biblical text, looking particularly to the teaching of Ignatius of Loyola on imaginative immersion in the narratives of Scripture. We then turn to the ancient practice of *lectio divina,* rooted in the Benedictine monastic tradition, which engages our *cognition* of the Bible through the faculties of memory and reason. After that we look at classical Christian teaching on holiness and virtue, summarized so adeptly by Thomas Aquinas, and reflect on the ways in which Scripture can help shape our *emotional* and behavioral life. Finally, we swim into the deep waters of the contemplative tradition as we consider how our reading of the Bible can realign the *intention* of our hearts and wills, drawing us into an ever deeper intimacy with God.

Readings

Legend tells that over the gateway to the sanctuary of Apollo, which in ancient times held the Delphic oracle, were inscribed the Greek words *gnōthi seauton:* know thyself. While self-absorption and navel-gazing are rarely helpful occupations, a little self-knowledge can be indispensable as we seek to orient our whole person toward life in Christ. As any physician will tell you, understanding how the various parts of a person fit and work together is essential if you want to make them (or keep them) fit and healthy.

The seven passages of Scripture below might help you reflect on the nature of a human person, especially that hidden, inner world we think of as the "soul" or "mind" or "heart." Remember that the Bible doesn't present a single, simple anatomical description of the soul, the way a medical textbook would describe the physical body. While these passages can offer us enlightening insights into our inner nature, we should be cautious about hardening those insights into a fixed, unalterable system. The model presented in this chapter is just that—a model—which can be helpful when used wisely, but it didn't come down from Sinai carved on stone tablets. The judicious person knows to apply an idea when it is helpful and set it aside when it no longer serves its purpose.

Day 1	Job 2:1-10	(Satan attacks Job's body, but not his spirit)
Day 2	Psalm 139:13-18	(the forming of the body)
Day 3	Ezekiel 37:1-10	(the valley of dry bones)
Day 4	1 Corinthians 15:35-49	(the body, before and after resurrection)
Day 5	2 Corinthians 6:14–7:1	(the body a temple of the Spirit)
Day 6	1 Corinthians 2:6-16	(spiritual knowledge)
Day 7	Romans 12:1-2	(offering ourselves to God)

8

LISTEN!

I eased the rental car along a narrow, hedgerowed lane under the shade of looming oaks overhead. Pheasants darted out of the undergrowth and across the road, all but throwing themselves under the wheels. I slowed to a crawl, winding with the road around the gentle contours of the north Yorkshire hillside until it finally broke free of the trees and a broad green valley opened up before me. In the distance a small scattering of red-roofed farmhouses were dwarfed by a complex of half-ruined buildings. Crumbling, pale sandstone walls glowed under the early morning sun. The verdant grass was broken here and there by the remains of tiled flooring. And soaring above it all was a congregation of delicate arches stretched toward heaven, seemingly weightless stone flung skyward and held in the skies by slender pillars, suspended in their own subtle tracery. I caught my breath in wonder. This was Rievaulx Abbey.

The valley around Rievaulx is idyllic. The modern visitor sees a landscape quite different from that settled by the founding Cistercian monks in the twelfth century, but even so the words of Walter Daniel, an early visitor to the site, still ring true:

The spot was by a powerful stream called the Rie in a broad
valley stretching on either side. . . . High hills surround the
valley, encircling it like a crown. These are clothed by trees
of various sorts and maintain in pleasant retreats the privacy
of the vale, providing for the monks a kind of second paradise of wooded delight. From the loftiest rocks the waters
wind and tumble down to the valley below, and as they make
their hasty way through the lesser passages and narrower
beds and spread themselves in wider rills, they give out a
gentle murmur of soft sound and join together in the sweet
notes of a delicious melody. And when the branches of lovely
trees rustle and sing together and the leaves flutter gently to
the earth, the happy listener is filled increasingly with a glad
jubilee of harmonious sound, as so many various things con-
spire together in such a sweet consent in music whose every
diverse note is equal to the rest.

The abbey at Rievaulx was one of the most important Cistercian
monasteries in medieval Britain, and for almost four centuries
played a central role in the spiritual life of northern England—and
far beyond. And at the heart of the monastic life in Rievaulx was a
determined pursuit of the presence of God through Scripture. While
darkness still swathed the valley, and the stars slowly turned overhead, the softly tolling bell would summon the brothers to matins.
Psalms were chanted by candlelight, punctuated by lengthy readings from the Bible and silence within which to digest them. For
many, a period of *lectio divina* would follow before sunrise. The
rhythm of the unfolding day continued to be marked by praying
Scripture; the offices celebrated under those magnificent arches
were abbreviated reminders of matins, also shaped around singing
psalms and listening for God's voice in short Bible readings.

I walked around the ruins, stopping to look through the doorway of the old refectory. Here the monks gathered to eat in silence

while one of the brothers read, perhaps from one of the prophets or a Pauline epistle. Further round the cloister the chapter house provided space for discussing abbey business and the practicalities of life in community; it was also a place for sharing together the practice of seeking God in the biblical text. (Bernard of Clairvaux's voluminous *Sermons on the Song of Songs*, recording his teaching at a sister Cistercian house, gives us an example of the nature of these conversations.) Over a doorway in the remains of a building on the south side of the complex were the worn remains of a sculpture: the annunciation of the birth of Christ to Mary by the angel Gabriel. The presence of the Bible was pervasive and inescapable. These medieval brothers must have been soaked in Scripture to a degree most of us would find unimaginable—and that immersion in the Bible drew them into an ever deeper immersion into the life of God.

Rievaulx Abbey

As I ambled round the site, soaking in the warmth of a beautiful summer's morning, I reflected that life in Rievaulx must have been glorious; secluded from the troubles of the world, communing with God in quiet prayer, absorbed in reading and meditation, drawing ever nearer to the divine. It seemed light years from my own experience—and perhaps yours. In our time, how many of us can enjoy the slow-paced reflective rhythm of a medieval monastery? A busy executive, pressured by targets, deadlines, budgets and the stress of office politics, has neither the time nor internal quiet to meditate throughout the day on the Bible. The mechanic unbending a fender in the body shop and the young mother besieged by feral preschoolers, both hedged in by incessant noise, can only dream of solitude and stillness. An elderly widower, held in his home by failing strength, might experience his isolation less as space for praying Scripture and more as a crushing burden of loneliness. Few of us, it seems, have the luxury of a life suited for contemplation.

But then, in reality, neither did the monks. Beyond the church and cloister, Rievaulx was a bustling center of activity. The land around the abbey was extensively developed for livestock, and sheep farming became an important industry for the brothers. Animal hides were tanned to make leather. The community developed mines for both lead and iron. There is even evidence that, near their woolhouse in Laskill, the monks developed an early (but very efficient) blast furnace for smelting the iron; after the dissolution of the monasteries under Henry VIII, nothing so technologically advanced would be seen for almost two centuries. Although we might picture an abbey like Rievaulx as a quiet, secluded center for contemplation, far removed from the activity of the world around, the truth was quite different. This community sought the presence of God in the midst of industry, commerce and political instability. If they were able to seek God in Scripture, and allow that searching to shape the course of their entire lives, so perhaps might we.

Paying Attention

If we truly desire to encounter God in Scripture on a regular, habitual basis in the midst of our frenetic and sometimes chaotic lives, we need first to cultivate the skill of maintaining a disciplined and sustained attentiveness toward God. Reading begins with perception, the ability to encounter Scripture to allow it to become internalized, part of our own minds and souls. This requires us to pay attention to the text, but even more so to pay attention to God who meets us in the text. This mindfulness of God is an unfamiliar practice to many of us in the contemporary Western church—and it is in precisely this area that we can learn so much from the example of the medieval monks like those at Rievaulx.

The monastic rule of St. Benedict, followed at thousands of communities like Rievaulx across the world, opens with a single word that encourages us from the very beginning to pay close attention to Christ: *Ausculta!* (*Listen!*) This attitude of the soul is emphasized repeatedly throughout the rule's prologue: "Listen carefully, my son, to the master's instructions, and attend to them with the ear of your heart. . . . Let us open our eyes to the light that comes from God, and our ears to the voice from heaven that every day calls out. . . . Let us listen well to what the Lord says." That opening *Ausculta!* set the tone for monastic life for the next millennium and a half, right up to the present day. Every action, every custom of monastic life was carefully and intentionally ordered to help the monk be more attentive to Jesus, to be able to incline a listening heart to his gentle voice.

The rule of Benedict itself overflows with examples. The liturgy centered on praying the Psalms because they were believed to represent the prayers of Jesus himself, who even now intercedes for us before his heavenly Father. To pray the Psalter was to learn to pray like Christ—with Christ, even. Obedience to the abbot gave opportunity to practice obedience to Jesus. Kitchen service emulated the foot washing Christ gave to his disciples. Even the hospitality offered to guests—for which Benedictines became so famous—was an exercise in loving Jesus through others, as Benedict wrote in his rule: "All guests who present themselves are to be welcomed as Christ."

It's important for us to notice that *every* aspect of life became an opportunity to practice attentiveness. Chanting psalms or praying in the oratory could clearly enable the fervent monk to soak himself in Christ. But Benedict, and the Benedictine tradition that developed from his rule, were very clear: cooking a meal, fixing fence posts, shearing sheep, balancing account books, teaching children, tending the sick—all of these, and every other imaginable everyday activity, also offer the chance to immerse ourselves in the presence of Jesus. The trick is simply paying enough attention, discovering how to be present to God in the moment.

Of course, that's easier said than done. It is not that God is reluctant to reveal himself to us—quite the opposite. Innumerable people throughout the history of the church have borne witness to the wide variety of ways in which God has lovingly made himself known. We may even have experienced in our own lives the gracious Spirit drawing back the veil between this world and the greater reality in which God dwells. But God desires more from us, for a deeper and intimate relationship that has to be founded on more than a few chance encounters of grace. God longs for us to be more consistently attentive.

When Moses was captivated by the burning bush, he wasn't cultivating a discipline of habitual attentiveness to God; his eye was caught by the sight of the flames and curiosity drew him closer in. But as his life with God deepened, so he sought to develop a more deliberate and sustained practice of seeking the presence of God. During the forty long years in which the Hebrews traveled between Egypt and the Promised Land, he purposefully erected a tent on the edge of the camp at every stopping place, calling it the "tent of meeting." Then day after day Moses would go out to this tent to meet with the Lord, to seek the face of the Holy One of Israel. The fire that animated the burning bush also burned here, but in a great pillar of flame and smoke that rested over the tent. The same voice spoke, but now not an unknown and unfamiliar voice; this was the voice of a constant companion, one who had made himself known. The book of Exodus tells us, "the LORD used to speak to Moses face to face, as one speaks to a friend" (Ex 33:11).

Inner and Outer Worlds

Is it possible for any of us to develop such deliberate and continual attentiveness? Isn't this the preserve of the mystics and hermits—like the monks at Rievaulx, for example—who have the time, space and inclination to immerse themselves in religious experience? Such people often seem to have a certain character, a particular personality that is rare and unusual. The rest of us live a slightly less elevated existence, rooted more in the bare earth than in the seventh heaven. Perhaps we're simply not wired to encounter God in such a personal and intimate way.

In our contemporary church culture, extroverts are in particular danger of being led to believe that a deep, rich, inner experience of God is simply beyond them. One of the better known, and most well established, categories in contemporary psychology is the scale of extroversion and introversion. It's also one of the most widely misunderstood distinctions. In the popular imagination, extroverts are the wild, fun-loving party animals, those who are most sociable, active and outgoing. In contrast, introverts are believed to be the quieter souls who keep their own company (sometimes to the point of being downright antisocial), the scholars, loners and contemplatives.

Although there's considerable truth in these generalizations, they don't quite hit the mark. Many extroverts are very sociable, but a handful are not. It's not at all unusual to find outgoing and expressive introverts. Many clergy, for example, are highly introverted, but it would be difficult to guess that while watching them enthusiastically leading worship and preaching on a Sunday morning. For a more accurate picture, start by thinking of a spectrum rather than two poles. Very few people are simply "extroverts" or "introverts"; we all lie somewhere on a line between those two extremes. Those toward either end of the line may fit the stereotyped pictures quite well. But many more of us, finding ourselves partway along the spectrum, will blend a little of both personality types, perhaps functioning now more as an extrovert and then more as an introvert. We are too complex simply to be slotted into one of two boxes.

Those who are more extroverted usually prefer to function in the external world, the universe *outside* their heads, sometimes through interaction with other people and at other times through physical activity. Extroverts are not typically drawn by their interior life, by reflection and the internal conversations of the mind; they prefer external stimulation. Some can find engaging with their inner world tremendously challenging, even painful and uncomfortable. The more introverted, on the other hand, much prefer to function in that inner world, the universe *inside* their heads. Depending on the nature of their introversion, they may experience the world around them as somewhat tedious or irrelevant or incomprehensible or threatening. As a result, they are typically content to live in a far greater degree of isolation from the outer world than extroverts could ever tolerate.

Of course, this means that in general extroverts tend to be a little more sociable, and introverts a little less so—after all, "other people" are part of the external world to which extroverts are drawn and which many introverts find so uncomfortable or tedious. But the stereotypes are riddled with exceptions. That lonely hiker may be an unsociable extrovert who loves the physicality of the natural world. The intense group sitting in conversation in the coffee shop may be deep introverts who are exploring the inner world of ideas together. The fundamental distinction which determines whether we are extroverts or introverts is not whether we are sociable or unsociable, lively or quiet, but whether we find the outer, physical world or the inner, intellectual world most stimulating and absorbing.

We might still expect, then, that introverts will more naturally and easily find themselves able to practice attentiveness to God. After all, they already value and enjoy solitude and reflection. The more introverted we are, the more ready we would seem to be to withdraw from worldly concerns, meditate on Scripture and enter a deep experience of contemplative prayer as we practice the presence of God. Maybe the introverts should seek to encounter God through Scripture, while the extroverts focus on organizing the softball team and going on preaching missions.

And that would be right, if the real issue at stake here were the ability to be quietly reflective, to dwell comfortably and silently in the realm of ideas and meditation. But that would be to presume that God were somehow more present to us in our inner world than in the outer world—an idea the Christian tradition has always vigorously rejected. Certainly we experience God in the hidden chamber of the spirit, the silent temple of the heart. But God is also made present to us in bread and wine, in the flowing water of baptism, in other human beings made in God's image, in the sweeping majesty of creation which declares God's "eternal power and divine nature" (Rom 1:20). In fact, as I have already said, the skill needed for an encounter with God is *attentiveness,* the ability to turn our hearts and minds fully in the direction of God (wherever he reveals himself) and keep them there. It is a skill that can be learned. And, surprisingly, it is a skill that is both equally accessible and equally difficult for extroverts and introverts alike.

Extroverts struggle to be attentive because they are so easily distracted by their external environment. Unable to keep themselves still for long, they are dazzled and drawn away by the bright lights, pulled into whatever excitement lays near at hand—a conversation, the football game, the great outdoors. Introverts, of course, have no such problem. Many of them can happily sit quietly for hours. But only let an introvert have a few moments alone and the distractions immediately flood in. Introverts have a vibrant inner landscape. Thoughts and feelings cascade over one another so quickly they can be hard to catch. A universe of ideas spins within them, a limitless cosmos grips their imaginations. Their bodies may be still as stone, but inside the soul is whirling. Certainly, God is present in both the extrovert's external world and the introvert's inner world. But all we see are the glittering, fascinating *distractions*. When it comes to sustaining focused concentration in one direction—on God himself—introverts are no more gifted than extroverts. Being attentive to the divine is hard for everyone.

The Butterfly Mind

However, we should not despair. Most of us find it difficult to pay attention to anything, whether to God or anything else. We have butterfly minds, constantly fluttering from one bright attraction to the next; the only difference between each of us is which distractions we find ourselves most drawn toward, and whether they are within us or in the outside world. So fixing our gaze on God and keeping it there is hard—but not impossible. Anyone (whether extrovert, introvert or some combination of the two) can learn to be more attentive and so more aware of God, and especially more alert to God's presence in Scripture. First, we need to learn basic skills that will help focus our attention. One that I have found particularly useful is breath counting.

How hard could it be to count your breathing? As I sit here, relaxed and therefore breathing quite slowly, I begin to pay attention to the simple movement of air into and out of my body. I breathe in, my lungs expanding a little, enjoying the sensation of the cool afternoon air being drawn in. *One.* My diaphragm pushes up marginally, and I exhale. There is a moment's pause, and then

I breathe in again. *Two.* Gently the air leaves my body again. How difficult could it be to count, say, ten of these breaths?

It turns out to be extraordinarily difficult. Difficult, that is, for my mind to count ten breaths *while doing nothing else.* It sounds so terribly easy, but in practice, it's hard to get past two or three breaths before my butterfly mind begins to flit to something more exciting. The exercise usually proceeds something like this. Breathe in. *One.* Breathe out. Notice ceiling fan spinning above me. Hear car passing on the street outside. Breathe in. Notice cell phone lying on the table. *Two.* Remember that I had meant to return a call before dinner. Who was I supposed to call? Something about the car? Breathe in again. Must have breathed out without noticing it. *Three.* Thinking about the car reminds me that I forgot to fetch groceries this morning. People are coming to stay this weekend, and we need more bread, milk and pasta. Perhaps a frozen pizza or two. Breathing in again. Did I miss one? Is that three or four now? Who did I mean to call? Perhaps I should start counting again. Breathe in. *One* . . .

If you want to experience the butterfly mind in action, count your breathing. Stop reading for a few seconds, sit still and try to count ten breaths, focusing on nothing but the breathing itself. You'll find the breathing is second nature, and the counting easy. But the attentiveness—well, that's something else entirely.

Breath counting is a very simple exercise you can practice almost anywhere and at practically any time. Waiting in a doctor's office, sitting on a bus, standing in line at the grocery store or drinking coffee in your kitchen in the early morning. Whenever you're not required to be concentrating on anything else, you can hone your concentration skill simply by paying attention to what your own body is doing. It's not a New Age meditation technique, an Eastern meditation practice or a yoga discipline. It's neither esoteric nor occult. It's just a little trick to encourage that butterfly to learn how to sit still once in a while.

The Practice of the Presence of God

Once we have begun to develop the skill of attentiveness, we can move on to another more fruitful exercise, often known as practicing the presence of God.

A little background might be helpful here. One winter's day in the early years of the seventeenth century a young man named Nicholas from Hériménil, in the French Duchy of Lorraine, stood contemplating a tree. Shivering in the cold air, he became fascinated as he studied the dry, barren branches. The tree gave every appearance of being dead. No movements, no fruit, no leaves. It seemed to reflect the bitter lifelessness of the snow-covered earth surrounding it. And yet, Nicholas reflected, it was far from dead. Buried in the heart of this tree—and the dozens of trees around it, and every meadow plant and hedgerow shrub—was an irresistible gift of life which would soon burst forth in fertile splendor. Somehow this tree spoke powerfully to Nicholas of the irrepressible and prodigal providence of God. As he stood watching the tree, he became alert to the presence of God.

The experience never left him. Within a very short time he had been drafted into military service during the Thirty Years' War then raging across central Europe. While fighting in a pitched battle near his hometown Nicholas received a dreadful leg injury that ended his career as a soldier—the painful wound was to plague him until his death. After recovering he spent some time acting as valet to a local nobleman. But his heart was being drawn in a different direction. Eventually he traveled to Paris and entered the priory of the Discalced Carmelites as a lay brother.

At the time, most monastic communities were divided into two main parts. The "choir monks" sang the daily offices in the oratory, spent extensive periods in meditation and prayer, and had opportunities to develop their education through reading and study. Lay brothers, on the other hand, were the domestic backbone of the community. They were expected to attend to the practicalities of life in community, leaving the choir monks free to pursue their more spiritual and intellectual calling. Lay brothers would farm, cook and clean. They were carpenters, plumbers, builders and maintenance workers. They were expected to pursue their much simpler prayers during the spaces in their daily routine of manual labor. They certainly were not expected to become spiritual giants.

Nicholas was assigned to the kitchens for the first fifteen years of his life as a Carmelite—an assignment he loathed. He was constantly moving about the kitchen, cooking, cleaning and fetching food from the stores, which caused excruciating pain in his wounded leg. On more than one occasion he was sent out of town to buy supplies, which was even more difficult; he later recalled how, while traveling back to Paris on one such trip on a barge loaded with barrels of wine, he could only move around the boat by rolling himself over the tops of the barrels. Eventually, as it became clear that he was simply unable to discharge his duties any longer, he was moved to the sandal workshop, where he was responsible for manufacturing and repairing the monks' footwear. Here, sitting at his bench all day long, he was much happier—and since the job entailed less constant physical labor, he was more able to receive visitors.

One of those visitors was a young French priest named Joseph de Beaufort. Over a period of a few years, Joseph had a number of conversations with Nicholas, who described to the priest something he called "the practice of the presence of God." Although during his years of service Nicholas had been able to spend little time in the oratory, or immersed in study of the Scriptures, he had nevertheless sought to become as aware of God's presence as he possibly could. God was present, he had found, in the kitchens and workshops as much as the chapel; it was simply a matter of paying attention. Just as in his youth he had waited patiently before the winter tree until God had revealed himself, so now he had learned to patiently seek God at all times and in all places. Joseph was captivated. He made notes on his conversations. He also gathered together letters Nicholas had written to other visitors at the priory, and a handful of short notes Nicholas had drafted out on this approach to prayer. He printed all these texts in a short book we now know as *The Practice of the Presence of God*—publishing them under the name Nicholas Herman had taken when he first entered the Carmelite priory so many years before: Brother Lawrence of the Resurrection.

In the two centuries since then Brother Lawrence's little book has sold millions of copies around the world and has become one of the most famous Christian classical spiritual writings of all time. Its secret lies in its simplicity. Unlike some of his fellow Carmelite writers, most notably John of the Cross and Teresa of Ávila, Brother Lawrence developed no comprehensive and systematic understanding of the contemplative life. He contributed very little to spiritual theology. He wrote no detailed treatises on stages in the life of prayer. He simply commended his simple idea of *practicing the presence of God*. He described it like this:

> In several books I found different methods to approach God and various practices of the spiritual life that I feared would burden my mind rather than facilitate what I wanted and what I sought, namely, a means of being completely disposed to God. This led me to resolve to give all for all. . . . I began to live as if only he and I existed in the world. Sometimes I considered myself before him as a miserable criminal at his judge's feet, and at other times I regarded him in my heart as my Father, as my God. I adored him there as often as I could, keeping my mind in his holy presence and recalling him as many times as I was distracted. . . . I was as faithful to this practice during my activities as I was during my periods of mental prayer, for at every moment, all the time, in the most intense periods of my

work I banished and rid from my mind everything that was capable of taking the thought of God away from me.

There is very little method here, more a determination to turn the heart toward God and keep it focused there. Lawrence would remind himself, wherever he was, that God was present. He would keep that idea fixed front and center in his mind. And then he would live in the light of that knowledge, doing everything for the love of God. Sometimes his sense of God's presence would be very strong, and at other times almost nonexistent. He paid little attention to this, but simply continued to live out the truth that God was near. Over time that sense of presence became more persistent and he became better at being attentive to it. He was less often practicing the presence and more often simply living it.

Exercises like breath counting help us to become more able to pay attention, to focus our concentration in a sustained way. Practicing the presence of God is no more than turning that sharpened attention toward God and keeping it there.

Slowing Down the Pace

Back in Rievaulx, I strolled south from the imposing pillars of the abbey church, around the east side of the cloister and into the grassed-over, roofless remains of the old scriptorium. Here the monks would have labored to produce the magnificent illuminated manuscripts which enabled the greatest literary works of the Western world (and a not inconsiderable number from the East) to be preserved and passed down through the centuries.

There were surprisingly few visitors that summer morning, and in the quiet peace it was easy to picture some young monk perched on a stool before his desk preparing to write. The writing of a single page required the investment of a great deal of time and effort. First the rough surface of the vellum needed to be scraped and rubbed smooth. Next the brother would mark out guidelines on the page along which to write, often by pricking small holes toward the edges of the page and tracing faint lines between them. If the page marked the opening of a book or chapter it would often warrant an elaborate illumination; in an important text (such as the Bible itself), not only would this illumination be colored but gold leaf might be delicately applied as a highlight. Then the text itself would be written—slowly, painstakingly, the brother constantly comparing his work with the source text as he dipped his pen into the ink, wrote a letter or two, dipped again, wrote another couple of letters and dipped into the ink again. He might invest the whole day in completing a single page of text; heavily illuminated pages would take even longer.

This necessary practice of book copying forced the monks to slow down and become deeply attentive to the text in hand—and, since they approached manuscript production as a devotional work, to become attentive to God in the text, especially when copying biblical texts. In our age we approach the Bible quite differently. We have cheap, convenient printed copies of Scripture that can be stuffed into our pockets or purses. We call up the Bible on our laptops and cell phones. With a quick search on the Internet and a cut, paste and print we can produce a fresh copy of a Gospel or an epistle. What for the medieval brother would have been the work of months is now just a short click away.

And we have become correspondingly inattentive to the text. We race through Scripture as though we were in the fast lane of the highway. Our eyes skip along the lines, half-remembering the phrases we feel we know so well. A young student is cramming his reading of the Bible into the few minutes before a lecture; needing a quick Scripture fix, he doesn't have time to slow down. The pastor in church is conscious that the clock is ticking; if he doesn't read the day's short passage quickly he'll have to cut back on the sermon. We no longer have anything as expansive as an attention span: we are seeking today's biblical sound bite.

So how can we become more attentive to the text and to the presence of God who comes to us through the text? How can we use our faculties of perception—our senses and imagination—to their fullest capacity as we encounter Scripture, so that we become as completely immersed in the Bible as is humanly possible? How can we learn to soak in Scripture until we are lost in its fathomless depths?

Readings

This week's readings help us to reflect on the constant presence of God around us, and our ability to be aware and attentive to that presence. It would be easy to allow these passages to lead us either toward theological speculations about the doctrine of God's omnipresence or into introspective soul-searching about whether we really are as attentive to God as we should be. While both avenues have their place, try to take a third road as you read this week. Allow the passages to speak to your heart—the heart in the biblical sense, the seat of your will and intention. Let the words draw your desire for God, your longing to be present to him as fully as possible, and your yearning to stretch into him through love.

Turn these passages into prayer. Let them open your soul to God, present with you as you read, so you can continue to seek and rest in his presence throughout the day that follows. You might find it helpful to journal not only about the readings themselves but also about your experience of developing attentiveness for God through the whole week.

Day 1	Psalm 139:5-12	(God is present everywhere)
Day 2	Psalm 73:21-26	(the faithfulness of God's presence)
Day 3	Proverbs 4:1-9	(listen to wisdom)
Day 4	1 Samuel 3:1-9	(Speak, LORD, your servant is listening)
Day 5	1 Kings 3:3-9	(Give me an understanding mind)
Day 6	John 10:1-5	(the sheep are attentive to the shepherd)
Day 7	Mark 13:33-37	(be alert, keep awake, watch)

9

LIVING IN THE GOSPEL

🜚

"So how did you get on this week?" Pat asked as she closed the folders on her desk and came to sit on one of the two armchairs in her small office.

"It was . . . different," I replied. "Surprising. It didn't go at all the way I expected." I looked over Pat's shoulder; outside the window a late spring snow was melting in the bright Colorado sun, icy water falling from budding branches into the warming soil.

She smiled but sat quietly, waiting for me to go on. Pat worked at a local Jesuit Retreat Center; over the years she had absorbed so much of the spirit and wisdom of the place that she now frequently directed people through the Ignatian Spiritual Exercises. I was one of a number of her directees. She was too shrewd to keep pushing the conversation; better to let the silence create space for thought and honesty.

I sipped from the mug of strong, black coffee cradled in my hands. "The reading from Matthew took an unexpected turn. I didn't finish it." Another brief silence. "This reading had touched me more deeply than I expected; I'm not reluctant to talk about it, but it's tricky finding the words."

Meditating on Matthew

Early in the morning, when I wasn't likely to be interrupted, I had gone down to my makeshift chapel, knelt at my prayer desk and opened up the Bible to the day's reading. Following the method of the Exercises, I began to picture the scene in my imagination. Jesus and his disciples were in some indefinite place in Galilee, probably traveling between towns. In my mind's eye I began to see Palestine in the first century—or, at least, what I imagined Palestine might have been like; I have no way of knowing quite how accurate my mental picture truly was. I pictured a bright, spring day, wisps of cloud scudding across an azure sky. Dust from the road was caught up in the slight breeze, and the broad leaves of the palms by the roadside rustled slightly. Jesus and the disciples were talking.

> When Jesus came into the district of Caesarea Philippi, he asked his disciples, "Who do the people say the Son of Man is?" And they said, "Some say John the Baptist, but others Elijah, and still others Jeremiah or one of the prophets." He said to them, "But who do you say that I am?" (Mt 16:13-15)

I imagined myself as part of the group of disciples, and as Jesus asked that question—"Who do you say that I am?"—it seemed as though he directed it not to Peter but straight at me. And immediately I knew what I wanted to answer.

My answer was not Peter's answer. I knew Peter's response well; I had studied it, analyzed it, preached it more than once. It was a good, solid, theologically precise answer, a profound confession of faith in Jesus as Messiah and Son of God. Those few short words bore an unimaginable weight of significance, leaning back into the heart of Jewish tradition and yet expressing the most startling affirmation of Jesus' divine nature. It was a great answer. But, I suddenly realized, it wouldn't have been my answer.

As soon as I heard Christ ask me the question, a response welled up from somewhere deep inside. "But who do you say that I am?" he asked me. And I replied, "You are beautiful."

It was such a deep, visceral response I couldn't deny it. But I had no idea why I answered in that way, nor why that response had risen up with such speed and emotional force. I needed time to think this through. For the next few days I returned over and again to that prayer experience, trying to fathom what had happened. Now, trying to describe it to Pat, I felt no nearer to understanding.

After a few moments of silence, she quietly asked me, "Well, have you asked the Lord about this?"

I felt so stupid. You'd think it would be obvious: if you don't understand what you've experienced with Christ in prayer, come back again and ask him. But it was taking time for such a simple idea to settle into my thick skull; I have a tendency to live in my head, and although I have enjoyed deep and wonderful experiences with God from time to time, I've always taken them away to some quiet place to work through in my own mind. During the Exercises I had begun to learn that Christ offers me his mysteries not as puzzles to solve but as enticements to come back for more.

So I took a moment to pray. Lord, why *did* I say that? I've studied so much theology, spent so many years teaching and preaching—why didn't I have a more philosophical and thoughtful answer? "You are beautiful"—where did that come from?

And as I asked, I suddenly understood. Whether the Spirit spoke to me or simply nudged something within my heart, I'm not sure. There were no voices or visions. But immediately I knew why I had answered that way. For me, beauty is what gives the world meaning and value. I don't have much ambition or desire for wealth, but I'm easily entranced by the beautiful. My wife is very relational, so when I want to offer her a compliment I know *she'll* appreciate I tell her she's the world's most wonderful wife and mother. But when I want to say something that means a great deal to *me*, I tell her she's beautiful. It's my highest compliment: you embody all that makes life worth living.

"You are everything," I said quietly. Pat looked at me quizzically. "You are everything," I repeated. "That's what I was saying. Take beauty out of my world and you've ripped the heart from it. And he is so beautiful. Without him, without his beauty, life would become tasteless and empty. He is beautiful, and so he is everything."

Pat picked up the Bible from her desk and turned to the passage from Matthew. She ran a finger down the page, past Peter's answer ("You are the Messiah, the Son of the living God!") and on a few verses. Jesus told Peter that he, Jesus, must suffer and die at the hands of the priests and elders in Jerusalem. Peter was appalled: "God forbid it, Lord! This must never happen to you!" The pain, the outrage in his voice is almost palpable.

Pat closed the Bible and looked me in the eyes. "Don't you think that when Peter gave his brilliant theological response, he might simply have been saying, 'You are everything'?" she asked. "Perhaps your answers weren't so different after all."

She was right. At that moment I realized I hadn't studied the passage, analyzed the grammar, teased out the theological truths. I had *lived* the story. Through the Gospel words I had been brought into the presence of Christ. The living presence of God had broken through the lifeless page. Narrative had become conversation.

Ignatius of Loyola

This was precisely the kind of engagement with Scripture that Ignatius of Loyola, the founder of the Society of Jesus, sought to encourage when he composed his famous Spiritual Exercises in the early sixteenth century. Ignatius himself was drawn to the world of the Bible in a rather unique way. Born into a wealthy and noble Basque family, in his late teenage years he (like many young men of his rank in society) took up military service, fighting with distinction in a number of battles over the next two or three years.

But during a siege of the Navarrese city of Pamplona he was struck in the legs by a cannonball; one leg was gruesomely wounded and the other badly broken. Carried back home to his family castle, he spent a number of painful months immobilized while his wounds slowly healed.

During his convalescence he read voraciously, and after a while stumbled across a book by Ludolph of Saxony called *The Life of Christ*. Ludolph had collected passages from some of the greatest Christian writers (such as Augustine of Hippo and Gregory the Great) to retell the gospel story of Christ's life. He encouraged his readers to savor each of the stories in turn, taking time to imagine that they were present at each of the events described—to picture themselves at the stable in Bethlehem or watching the loaves and fishes being shared around the great crowd or standing at the foot of the cross. For months Ignatius immersed himself in the Gospel narratives and, as his body gradually recovered, so he found his soul gradually reformed and renewed by the experience of being so entirely steeped in Scripture.

After his recovery Ignatius was fired with a desire to help others discover the treasure of the Bible. This was the genesis of the Society of Jesus, the religious order known to most of us as the Jesuit fathers. Ignatius and his companions fanned out across Europe and beyond (some of the earliest missionaries to the recently discovered "New World" of the Americas were Jesuits) with one single burning passion: to help people know Christ through Scripture. The Spiritual Exercises became their handbook and guide (and still is to this day). The short book, a manual for spiritual directors, describes a structured program for slowly and prayerfully reading the Gospels and finding ways of encountering the living Christ through his living Word.

The basic method of the Exercises is very simple. Ignatius would encourage people to begin by paying attention to every detail of a Gospel story: the setting, the people involved, gestures and words, the time of day or year. He would teach them to use their imagination to recreate the scene in their minds, making it as present to the senses as possible—if you were there, what would you see? What might you hear? What fragrances drift through the air? Is it warm or cold, wet or dry? Who is gathered around you? What are they doing? Where is Jesus in this story, what is he doing, and how are others reacting? We might imagine a director preparing to shoot a scene for a movie. In his mind he has to consider every detail. How will this scene look and feel? What movements are required? What dialogue will take place? The director has to become supremely attentive to detail—and so must we, Ignatius might add.

Then, following the teaching he had received from Ludolph's book, he would encourage people to insert themselves into the scene. Don't just watch; participate. Can you imagine yourself as a disciple or a person in the crowd? As a leper or blind man, a sinful woman or righteous Pharisee? What is it then like, experiencing these unfolding events? If, in your imagination, you are no longer a passive observer but an involved actor in the scene, how does it affect your perception of the story? In particular, Ignatius counseled his directees to pay close attention to their emotions: what do you feel? Our emotional responses often give us important clues about the way the story is directly touching us—where we struggle with or rejoice in the gospel message. They may shape the way we want to respond to what Jesus is doing, even taking the story off in unexpected directions. We might be praying through the story of Jesus meeting a paralyzed man beside the pool in Jerusalem (Jn 5:1-9). Jesus approaches the man and asks him, "Do you want to be made well?" The man, of course, responds affirmatively. But we may be surprised, imagining ourselves in his place, to find that we are resisting Jesus, holding him at arm's length, uncertain whether we want his healing in our lives. We have allowed the story to unearth something deep within, something which can now become the focus of our prayer.

And that's precisely where Ignatius would have guided people next: into prayer. Each of the Exercises concludes with what Ignatius called a "colloquy," a spiritual conversation. But Ignatius taught people to allow the meditation and conversation to blend together in the context of the imaginative engagement with the Gospel story. To continue the example, we might have pictured ourselves as the lame man lying beside the pool, asked by Jesus if we truly want to be healed. We want to explore our reaction to that invitation more fully with Christ. Ignatius urges us not to break the meditation, to step out of the scene in order to pray. We have pictured ourselves in the presence of Christ: from within that scene, speak with Christ. As you lay beside the Jerusalem pool, talk with Jesus "exactly as one friend speaks to another," as Ignatius expressed it. Allow the conversation to develop as a natural extension of the meditation. And then listen. Be ready to hear Christ's response.

It's precisely at this point that some of us experience an important difficulty: if I'm imagining this scene, and imagining speaking to Christ, am I not simply imagining his response? In other words, I could "hear" Jesus speaking to me, but wouldn't I just be making it up? Isn't this simply self-delusion, pretending that I can put words into Jesus' mouth?

There are those who hold that God speaks to us today in no other way than through the written words of Scripture, and such people will never be able to understand this practice as anything other than a delusional game. But many of us believe that God continues to speak to his people directly and personally—in a way consistent with Scripture certainly, but not only through the book itself. We may have experienced this in a variety of ways: a vague sense that God is "nudging" us to do or say something; a feeling that God is speaking to us through the words of some poem, book, song or conversation; a clearer perception that God is present in some place; even (from time to time) the unmistakable experience of "hearing" the voice of God—although for most of us that last phenomenon is rare indeed. We are, in principle at least, open to the idea that Christ might speak to us. But we want to be able to distinguish clearly between the genuine voice of God and "just imagining." Doesn't an Ignatian colloquy lead us exactly where we don't want to be—into the heart of our imagination?

The simple answer is yes. But before we dismiss Ignatius out of hand, we might want to stop and explore whether that really is such a problem.

Spiritual Vision

In Western culture most people have come to see the imagination as frivolous, playful and essentially disconnected from the real world. In ancient times people greatly respected (even feared) their dreams, seeking to listen to the voice of their imagination by night; we dismiss our dreams as the product of stress, stimulation or overindulgence in cheese. Daydreaming and fantasizing are equated with wasting time and laziness. When others' ideas seem disconnected from worldly reality we say, with an ironic tone, that they have a "vivid imagination." The implication is clear: the imagination may be creative and entertaining, but it cannot be trusted. It is a purely internal playground where we can indulge our fantasies without consequence; to take it too seriously would be foolish and risky.

In previous generations, however, Christians took a much more positive view of the imagination: it was seen as the soul's equivalent of the body's physical senses. The imagination had a number of functions: it was the place where the information gathered by our five senses could be integrated and processed; the place where we could freely experiment with the store of ideas, concepts and memories held in our minds—and also as the primary gateway of spiritual experience. Traditionally Christians have assumed that

we become open to spiritual reality primarily through the imagination, which is capable of receiving experiences that are incomprehensible to our physical senses.

Think of Ezekiel's vision beside the river Chebar. In the midst
of a great storm cloud he saw multifaced living creatures, their
four wings outspread, surrounding a burning fire around which
sparks and lightning flashed. Beside the creatures were wheels
within wheels, their rims circled with eyes; the wheels turned to
and fro, rising and falling with the winged creatures. Over the
heads of the creatures Ezekiel saw a crystal dome, over which was
a sapphire throne on which was seated some kind of human figure
who seemed wrapped in fire.

How did Ezekiel see this? It seems fairly clear that this was a
visionary experience, not something he saw with his physical
eyes. Traditionally Christians would have interpreted this as God
revealing himself to Ezekiel through the imagination. We might
be tempted to ask, "So, Ezekiel was just imagining this?" But the
question would have made little sense to our ancestors in the faith.
Just imagining? Do you just see this book? Can you just smell your
coffee, or just hear the traffic? Your perception of those things
through your senses does nothing to undermine their reality. Why
do we assume that our imagination is so closed to God and to the
spiritual world that it can "only imagine" and never experience for
itself? Ezekiel didn't just imagine the vision of God: he saw it! The
fact that he saw it in his imagination made it no less real.

In the same way it is possible for Christ to speak to us in our
imagination—the real and actual living Christ truly and directly
speaking, not just in some fantasy. In fact, Ignatius is teaching us
an incredibly powerful way of opening ourselves to God's presence through Scripture. When we engage so intentionally with the
Bible in our imagination, we open ourselves more fully (not less)
to the spiritual reality of God's presence. It becomes easier for God
to speak into our minds, hearts and lives, not harder. Those who

have practiced the kind of biblical meditation Ignatius taught know the truth of this for themselves. It is possible for us to deceive ourselves, to play pretend, to put words into Christ's mouth. But, on the whole, we know when we are doing it. When I have a conversation with a friend, I can without difficulty discern the difference between what he is actually saying and what, in my mind, I wish he were saying. It is no harder to discern the difference between my fantasies about what Christ might say to me and the reality of Christ speaking. The psalmist wrote:

> The voice of the Lord is powerful;
> > the voice of the Lord is full of majesty. . . .
> The voice of the Lord flashes forth flames of fire.
> The voice of the Lord shakes the wilderness. (Ps 29:4, 7-8)

Those with experience know that the voice of God has an unmistakable and undeniable quality. If God speaks, you will know.

Exploring the Exercises

Learning to read Scripture like this takes practice and time. Ignatius created a month-long retreat during which he would counsel people to meditate and pray for a number of hours every day; many Jesuit retreat centers still offer these thirty-day retreats, and if you are one of the few people who is able to take four weeks out of a busy schedule you might want to consider attending such a retreat—it will change your life forever. But Ignatius recognized that most people would never be in a position to devote such an extended time to the Exercises, so he developed an alternative approach which encouraged people to meditate and pray for around an hour a day over the course of many months; this has become known as the "exercises in daily life."

Again, many Jesuit centers offer directors who would be willing to guide you through these Exercises; I can testify from my own experience to their life-transforming effect. But it is quite possible for you to begin praying Scripture in this imaginative and meditative way right now, wherever you find yourself, even if you have no guide or spiritual director to walk the journey with you. You have Scripture, and you have Christ. That is all you need.

If you want to explore this biblical prayer more fully, I would advise setting aside a reasonable period of time on a regular basis—at least half an hour every day would be best. But do be flexible and allow yourself grace; some people's circumstances will not allow even this (a single working mother in a noisy apartment building might be grateful to carve out fifteen minutes two or three times a week). Find what time you can, and offer it expectantly to God.

Settle yourself somewhere quiet where you are unlikely to be disturbed. Turn to a passage of Scripture on which to meditate. The seven passages listed at the end of this chapter, drawn from the heart of Jesus' life and ministry, might be an excellent place to start. After you become more familiar with this approach to reading and praying, you may want to branch out into more challenging areas of the Gospels, such as the passion narratives (the final chapters of each Gospel that tell the stories leading up to the crucifixion).

Follow the steps outlined below as you pray the passage:

- Imagine the scene as clearly and vividly as you can. Involve all your senses; imagine sounds, smells, even taste and touch.

- Allow yourself to be drawn into the scene as you imagine it. Place yourself in the shoes of one of the characters—a member of the crowd, an onlooker, a disciple, a questioner or a sick person lying before Christ.

- Allow the events of the narrative to run through your mind, and pay attention to the details of what people say and do.

- Pay attention to your reactions. What feelings are stirred up as you experience this Gospel story? How do you want to respond to Jesus' questions and challenges?

- At some point (whether in the midst of the story or at the end) allow your reactions to become the starting point of a conversation with Christ. Speak "as one friend speaks to another." Listen carefully and attentively for his response, trusting that Christ truly longs to speak with you.

It is entirely possible to practice this meditative reading with any passage of Scripture, of course, whether it be Romans, Leviticus, Revelation or Isaiah. Personally, I have found the Song of Songs (which we read and prayed through earlier) to be a particularly rich text for such imaginative prayer. But it is much easier to begin with the Gospels before launching out into the rest of the Bible; it is easier to engage in the colloquy with Christ when we already have a clear sense of his presence in the narrative. As you become more adept at praying the Gospels, you will begin to understand how other biblical passages might be similarly prayed. Over time, you will learn the art of being ever more attentive to God in Scripture.

Readings

Using the Ignatian approach to praying with the Gospels described in this chapter, this week we are going to meditate on seven stories from the biblical accounts of the life of Jesus. It may be that you find one or more of these readings particularly fruitful—somehow, the story speaks powerfully into your life, stirs up unexpected emotions or responses, or brings you deeply into the presence of Christ. If so, stay with it, if necessary for the whole week. There are no rewards or prizes for completing all the passages; you can always come back to those you miss at a later date.

Ignatius encouraged making "repetitions" of our readings in this way. We are not seeking merely to consume the book, working our way through as many pages as we can in the shortest possible time. We are seeking God. So when Scripture brings us into an encounter with God, we would be wise to stay there. After all, wouldn't it be better to invest an entire year in reading a single verse well than in reading the whole Bible badly?

Day 1	John 2:1-11	(the wedding at Cana)
Day 2	Matthew 8:23-27	(Jesus calms the storm)
Day 3	Matthew 15:21-28	(the Syrophoenician woman)
Day 4	Mark 10:46-52	(blind Bartimaeus)
Day 5	Matthew 19:16-30	(the rich young man)
Day 6	Matthew 14:13-21	(the feeding of the five thousand)
Day 7	Matthew 17:1-9	(the transfiguration of Jesus)

10

THE BOOK OF CHRIST

Brother Matthew was solemnly professed in a strip mall. I had gathered with the other members of our community of the Grey Robe Monks of St. Benedict in a small church in the mall nestled between a Chinese restaurant and a burger bar. Outside a glass-fronted door at the back of the sanctuary a group of three young men were standing around beside the dumpster, sucking down bottled beer and talking animatedly, the cigarettes in their gesturing hands leaving smoky trails in the air. In the church we watched the prior invite Brother Matthew to formally declare his desire to be received into the community under lifelong vows, rather than the "simple" vows he was already under (which last only for a single year). Matthew read the declaration, then prostrated himself face down on the floor in front of the altar, arms outstretched on the ground as though he were about to be crucified. Two brothers came forward carrying a pall, the large richly decorated cloth that is traditionally draped over the coffin during a funeral. They drew the pall over Matthew's body and knelt beside him as one of the sisters stepped forward and began to lead us in a long, slow, haunting chant.

Matthew was dying.

Not literally dying—or, at least, not physically, which may not amount to the same thing. This ceremony was a ritual death, a symbolic departure from the life Matthew had lived until this moment. Like baptism, this ancient monastic liturgy enabled Matthew to identify with the cross and resurrection of Christ, letting go of life in order to receive the gift of new life. Watching the brothers drape the pall over him, listening to the melancholy tones of the Gregorian melody, looking into the somber faces of the brothers and sisters gathered around him—all this was intensely and profoundly moving. There was more taking place here than met the eye, more than simply a man lying on the ground while others sang. This liturgy carried more weight, more meaning.

Under the pall, Brother Matthew began to tremble. Like a bride at the altar or a soldier climbing down into a foxhole, he began to realize with unnerving clarity the reality and significance of what was happening. As the chant drew to a close, the two kneeling brothers stood and drew back the pall, allowing Brother Matthew to raise himself to his knees and read the vow of solemn profession. The words of the vow were uncomplicated and written in large, clear type on a card held before him, yet he stumbled and stuttered through them. Lying under that deathly cloth had shaken him, shattered his nerves, or perhaps he truly was a man newly born, still wrestling to command his faculties. Either way, all of us gathering in that room understood his struggle. We too had been gripped by the profundity of the moment.

Brother Matthew rose shakily to his feet to be embraced by the prior, a look of joy and relief on his face. I watched, thoughtful. As a brother in simple vows in this order, I would make the same profession in another year or two. I would lie under that pall, listening to the community mournfully sing as I relinquished life. Soon, I too would die.

Experiencing the ritual had changed my perspective. What had previously been rubrics on the page of a prayer book had become a stark reality. The seeming simplicity of the words of the vows had been replaced by a sense of the radically transformed way of life those words implied. Clearly, there was more to all this than I had first realized.

Changed Perspectives

If the whole of Scripture is going to become for us a place of encounter with Christ, we may need to experience a similar shift of perspective. After all, Jesus doesn't even seem to appear as a character in the biblical story until somewhere around the thousandth page. Almost four-fifths of the narrative of the Bible is over before we ever get to the stable at Bethlehem. It seems easy enough to imaginatively meditate on the Gospels, as I described in chapter nine, in order to meet with Jesus. But what are we to do with Leviticus or Ecclesiastes or Lamentations? Many of our Bibles are far more well-thumbed in the New Testament and, perhaps, Isaiah and the Psalms—the most obviously Jesus-centered parts of Scripture. How are we to dive into the rest?

Perhaps we need a fresh viewpoint. It's often the case that some experience, event or piece of knowledge can shift our perspective in a significant way. We interpret a friend's apparently uncharacteristic behavior in a new light when we discover he's recently fallen in love. Visiting the country in which a favorite movie is set helps us understand the story in a fresh way. Seemingly erratic decisions being made in the workplace make sense when we learn that the company is being subjected to a hostile takeover. In each case, a broader understanding of the context leads to enhanced comprehension.

This also happens every time we read a detective story or a mystery novel. At first we are confronted with a seemingly unfathomable sequence of events: some violent crime, perhaps, or a spectacular theft. A diverse collection of characters are caught up in the orbit of these events, each with their own peculiarities and problems. We know, as we read, that at least one of these people is involved in this crime—perhaps some shocking murder—but which one? And how? As their tangled tales begin to unravel we find ourselves suspecting first one person, then another; in a well-written novel (rather unlike real life) we may eventually find that almost everyone has had the motive and opportunity to commit the murder, and the complexity is overwhelming. But the great detective, of course, is not as nonplussed as we are. Just when everything seems insoluble a revelation strikes as some vital clue is uncovered. The final scene is set and in a dramatic denouement the detective unmasks the villain, showing how the trail of evidence leads uniquely to him or her, while explaining all the red herrings and blind alleys. And we, hopefully, close the book with a feeling of rich satisfaction, nodding sagely as we say to ourselves, "Of course—it all makes sense!"

Now imagine going back to the book for a second time. Returning to the first page, we already know how the entire story will unfold. When we first meet the murderer, we know he is the murderer. At the first mention of a vital clue, we already know its significance. Hints are dropped about dark secrets—but we already know what those secrets are. For us, the whole book has changed. The story still unwinds along the same course; the detective still reaches the same conclusions. But our reading is so different. Events and remarks we hadn't noticed the first time take on a fresh significance. Characters emerge in a new light. We have been given an oracular knowledge: we still may not understand everything, but we have seen enough of the way this story unfolds to grasp it more fully than those who participate in it. We see what the detective and the other characters cannot see, what even a first reader of the text cannot see. We have the key.

What if we could read Scripture in this way? This was the beguiling idea which enchanted the minds of some of the greatest thinkers, writers and biblical scholars in the history of the church.

And no one articulated the ideas that lay at the heart of their thinking more compellingly than a young Scottish priest named John Duns Scotus.

The Absolute Primacy of Christ

In the closing years of the thirteenth century John made his way to the university at Oxford to teach theology and philosophy. The Oxford of his day was, of course, quite different from the city modern visitors see. Although John was arriving in one of the foremost cities of England, strategically situated at the heart of the country, it would seem to us little more than a village. As Oxford eased into the fourteenth century (unaware of the horrors that war and plague were shortly to bring) it boasted fewer than fifteen hundred buildings (including the churches, monasteries and college properties) huddled in a few streets in the shadow of the Norman castle; there were probably not many more than two thousand residents all told. Most people, including the university students, were housed in wood-frame, thatched roof homes, which were drafty, dark and infested with rodents. The half dozen or so colleges then in existence were small institutions largely devoted to the study of Latin, theology and philosophy (many graduates would be drawn into the service of the church), and were dominated by the newly arrived Dominican and Franciscan friars. The "dreaming spires" celebrated by the poet Matthew Arnold were only just beginning to rise, and most lay decades or even centuries into the city's architectural future. But Oxford's reputation as a leading center for both learning and teaching was already firmly established. Considered to be on par with such luminary institutions as the universities of Paris or Bologna, it drew some of the greatest thinkers in western Europe.

Even in this rarified atmosphere, John quickly established himself as one of the most brilliant minds of his generation. Probably only in his early thirties when he began giving lectures—

maybe even his late twenties—he showed a precocious genius for philosophical analysis. His ability to work with the most obscure and abstract concepts, to draw keen distinctions and to develop a wide-ranging web of ideas into a complex but coherent philosophy later earned him the nickname *Doctor Subtilis*, the "subtle doctor"—a name not always applied in a complimentary fashion. John could be so hard to follow, some of his later critics convinced themselves that his apparently impenetrable writing was simply a smokescreen covering the mundane thinking of a mediocre mind. But history judged them to be wrong. John Duns Scotus is now celebrated as one of the most fascinating, if difficult, of all medieval thinkers.

Among the contemporary theological questions that fascinated John was this: Why did Christ become a human being? (That's a question which may not seem to have much to do with reading and interpreting the Bible—but, as we shall see, the implications of John's response cut right to the heart of the way we approach Scripture.) Thirteen hundred years before John began teaching, a Jewish child had been born in the most humble of circumstances in the back streets of Bethlehem, itself an insignificant town in a minor Roman province. For centuries the Christian church had taught that this child was God incarnate, the immeasurable deity responsible for all creation somehow compressed into a tiny human form. What could possibly have motivated God to take such an extraordinary step: to allow himself to become so vulnerable, so limited, so small? Of all the ways God could have chosen to interact with humanity, why this one?

Two centuries before John, the scholar Anselm of Canterbury had written what came to be seen as a textbook answer to this question, in a dissertation titled *Cur Deus Homo?* or *Why Did God Become Human?* Anselm's arguments would sound familiar to many contemporary Christians. He began with the Fall: since our rebellion in Eden and the irruption of sin into this world, human beings are in desperate need of a Savior. Drawing on a line of thought which went back to the earliest church fathers, Anselm said that such a Savior would need to work within the confines of the world he sought to save and would have to assume the form of the creatures he wished to redeem. Fallen human beings can only be saved by the willing sacrifice of a perfect human being; God himself chose to become human in order to make that sacrifice, in the person of Christ on the cross. In short, Anselm said, Jesus came on a rescue mission to save the lost.

But John profoundly disagreed. Not with every part of Anselm's thinking: he didn't take issue with the idea that Jesus' sacrificial death on Calvary brought salvation for humanity. But he did question Anselm's ideas about what *motivated* God to become human in the first place. How is it possible, John asked, that the most wonderful event in human history—when God stepped into the material cosmos in physical form, sharing our life with us, revealing himself to us as never before, coming into close communion with ordinary people in a way they could never have imagined—how could this magnificent intervention into history have been prompted solely by the most appalling and degrading human truth: our utter sinfulness? How could the greatest good be caused by the greatest evil? To believe that Jesus came and saved sinners is a central Christian doctrine, John said. But to believe that he came only because we had sinned is monstrous. It suggests that we somehow forced God's hand, cornering him by our depravity into his single most beautiful expression of love.

John retold the human story theologically from a very different angle. His starting point was an idea known to us as the "absolute primacy of Christ." It's rather like a sophisticated version of the classic children's Sunday school credo: no matter what the question is, the answer is probably Jesus. John looked at the entire universe and the great sweep of history across the millennia, and began with a simple assumption: this is all about Christ.

All creation was made for Christ, John taught, echoing an idea
we already find in Paul's earliest letters: "in [Christ] all things in
heaven and on earth were created . . . all things have been created
through him *and for him*" (Col 1:16, emphasis added). The author
of Proverbs expresses the same idea in vibrant poetry (writing
about the personified figure of Wisdom, seen in the Christian tradition as a figure of Christ):

> When he established the heavens, I was there,
>   when he drew a circle on the face of the deep,
> when he made firm the skies above,
>   when he established the fountains of the deep,
> when he assigned to the sea its limit,
>   so that the waters might not transgress his command,
> when he marked out the foundations of the earth,
>   then I was beside him, like a master worker;
> and I was daily his delight,
>   rejoicing before him always,
> rejoicing in the inhabited world
>   and delighting in the human race. (Prov 8:27-31)

And from the beginning, John asserted, it was God's intention
that Christ should take human form, living among those in whom
he so delighted and participating directly in the created order. For
this reason this world was shaped as a place in which Christlike
life would flourish, where the "image" and "likeness" of God (Gen
1:26) would be most at home—an image and likeness most fully
seen in Jesus, who is supremely the "image of the invisible God"
(Col 1:15).

But there is an important implication in all this: there was always going to be an incarnation. Human sin changed the nature of
that divine participation: certainly without the Fall there would
have been no need for the brutal events of Good Friday. But our
brokenness did not provoke Bethlehem. Sin is not the fundamen-

tal fact of the universe, the primal reality of our existence. Christ is the foundation, the Alpha and Omega, the beginning and the end. The cosmos is shaped around Jesus. We are made in his image. He is the determining force behind all reality, all history, our entire human experience. And he is the goal, the destination, the endpoint toward which all history tends. In short, said John, Jesus is everything.

Christ in All Scripture

If, as John argued, the whole of creation entirely centers on Jesus, then we might reasonably expect to discover that Scripture is equally Christocentric. Not only that, but the idea of the absolute primacy of Christ could then become a compelling starting point for our interpretation of Scripture, especially when we approach Scripture with the desire, above all else, to find in it an encounter with God in Christ.

And in fact this was the way most Christians read the Bible for much of the church's two-millennia-long history (and for centuries before John was around to give such a strong theological foundation for the idea). During one of his sermons on the Psalms, the fifth-century African bishop Augustine of Hippo exhorted his congregation to "remember that God speaks only a single word throughout the length of Scripture, and that only one Word is heard from the many mouths of the sacred writers—the Word that was in the beginning, God with God." Six centuries later the hugely influential Parisian abbot Hugh of St. Victor would write: "All sacred Scripture is but one book, and that one book is Christ, because all divine Scripture speaks of Christ, and all divine Scripture is fulfilled in Christ."

These writers were developing a tradition that reaches right back to the New Testament period. Throughout the Gospels, the Epistles and the book of Revelation we see Jesus presented as the fulfillment of the Hebrew Scriptures. We have often narrowed that

focus by affirming that in Christ a specific collection of ancient
biblical prophecies about the future came to pass; some even claim
to be able to enumerate the number and sequence of such prophecies. But the apostles and the New Testament writers asserted so
much more: for them, Jesus was the completion and fulfillment of
all Scripture, of the whole Bible in its many varied aspects.

Think, for example, of Peter's first sermon on the day of Pente-
cost. These few brief words draw together a collection of different
texts from the Hebrew Bible—a passage from Joel and quotations
from a couple of psalms—and apply them all to Jesus. Two chapters later in Acts, Peter is confronting the Sanhedrin and quotes
from another Psalm ("the stone that the builders rejected has become the chief cornerstone" [Ps 118:22]) which, he asserts, speaks
directly of Christ. In a prayer later in the same chapter the disciples apply yet another Psalm to Jesus, while in chapter seven Ste-
phen, during his trial, draws whole sweeps of the Old Testament
narrative into his interpretation of the significance of Christ's
death and resurrection. Philip hears an Ethiopian official reading
from the book of the prophet Isaiah while traveling on the road to
Gaza and "starting with this scripture, he proclaimed to him the
good news about Jesus" (Acts 8:35). This same pattern continues
throughout Acts: the Old Testament is constantly referred to as a
text that speaks of Christ.

If anything, the picture becomes even richer as we turn to the
New Testament letters. Paul, in particular, seems to see Jesus
everywhere he looks in Scripture. Christ is portrayed as a new Adam,
a descendant of the first man who overturns the tragic results of
the first sin in Eden (Rom 5:12-21). Abraham's unwavering faith in
God's promise makes him the spiritual ancestor of those who will
place their faith in Christ's resurrection (Rom 4:1-25). Sarah and
Hagar become allegories of the challenging choice presented by
Christ: between living under the law of Sinai or in the freedom of
the new Jerusalem (Gal 4:21–5:1). In one text Jesus is linked to the

entire story of the exodus—to the "baptism" in the Red Sea, the leadership of Moses, the miraculous food and drink provided in the wilderness—leading to the startling assertion that Jesus was present to the Israelites throughout their wanderings: "they drank from the spiritual rock that followed them, and the rock was *Christ*" (1 Cor 10:4, emphasis added). And so it continues throughout Paul's letters—it seems that he is able to discern the presence of Christ in almost any biblical text.

The letter to the Hebrews draws on the Old Testament in a remarkable way to expound the significance of Christ's life, death and resurrection. After a short, breathless introduction in the first four verses (just a single sentence in the Greek original) the letter launches into a whirlwind tour of the Hebrew Scriptures: quotations from right across the Psalter; excerpts from books as diverse as Deuteronomy, Proverbs, Isaiah and Jeremiah; allusions to the meeting between Abraham and Melchizedek; the giving of the law at Sinai; Israel's wandering in the wilderness; the design and structure of the temple; the rules governing the priesthood and the sacrificial system laid out in Leviticus; and the prophetic promise of a new heart covenant between God and his people. The eleventh chapter famously presents a panorama of Old Testament heroes, calling to mind the examples of Abel, Enoch, Noah, Abraham, Isaac, Jacob, Joseph, Moses, Gideon, Barak, Samson— the list is overwhelming. And all this is offered as one great and glorious witness to Jesus, who is greater than the angels, who mediates a better covenant than Moses, who embodies the sabbath rest of the covenant, who fulfils the great priesthood of Melchizedek, who ministers in the true heavenly sanctuary of which the earthly temple is simply an imitation, who offers the supreme and final sacrifice, and who establishes the foundations of the heavenly Jerusalem.

No wonder, then, that the author of this letter calls Jesus "the pioneer and perfecter of our faith" (Heb 12:2). He is the beginning and the end, the one who participates in creation with God at the dawn of time and draws it to its conclusion at the end of days. His presence can be felt on every page, during every incident, through every prophecy, in every life. Jesus is not simply a character who appears in the Bible somewhere toward the end, drawing together the threads of a rambling and complex story. Jesus is the central character from the first page to the last. The Bible is, above all else, the book of Christ.

Readings

You may find it interesting and helpful to approach this week's readings using the same Ignatian method of meditation described in chapter nine. In each of these passages, drawn from the Old Testament, it is fairly easy to see a reflection of some part of the life and character of Jesus Christ—in Melchizedek's offering of bread and wine, for example, or Moses' transfiguration on the mountain.

As you meditate on each reading, allow yourself to become prayerfully aware of these parallels and connections, and be open to the possibility that Christ may be present to you in these narratives. Don't force it. If trying to see Jesus in these passages seems contrived, let it go—let God speak to you in whatever way he wishes through the words, and rest easy with that. Either way, journaling about your responses may help you come back and reflect at a later date.

Day 1	Genesis 14:17-20	(Abraham and Melchizedek)
Day 2	Exodus 34:29-35	(the shining face of Moses)
Day 3	Ruth 4:1-6	(Boaz redeems Ruth)
Day 4	1 Samuel 16:1-13	(David chosen as king)
Day 5	Proverbs 8:22-31	(Wisdom's role in creation)
Day 6	Isaiah 53:1-12	(the suffering servant)
Day 7	Zechariah 6:9-15	(the crowning of Joshua)

11

SACRED READING

r

The desert air was still cool as dawn broke over distant mountains to the west. Abba Anastasius, one of the hundreds of elderly monks scattered across the fourth-century Egyptian desert, pushed himself up from his reed mat bed, crossed himself, and stood in the doorway of his simple cell as he recited his familiar morning psalms by heart. As his prayer drew to a close he stayed in the doorway a moment longer, savoring the stillness of the wilderness and allowing himself to be cheered by the memory of the fervent monk who had visited him the day before. Such an eager young man! They had sat for hours discussing their prayer, their fasting and their experience of the spiritual life. The visitor had seemed especially delighted with Anastasius's Bible. Hardly surprising, of course; the hand-copied volume, a gift from a grateful nobleman, was worth a small fortune. Together they had pored over passages from the Psalter, the Gospels and two of Paul's letters, the young man's eyes sparkling as they read.

Anastasius stretched, went back into the cell and reached up to the shelf above the window for his precious text.

It was gone.

For a moment Anastasius could only stare up at the empty shelf in surprise. Then, slowly, realization washed over him. Only one person had enjoyed access to the cell the previous day: his enthusiastic visitor. The young man had left late the night before, and clearly the book had quietly departed with him.

The elderly monk went back to the doorway and sat down, looking out down the rough path leading up to his cell from the distant desert road. And he began to pray, singing softly to himself the psalms he had memorized from his beautiful book.

A few hours later the sun had climbed high in the sky, but still Anastasius sat praying in his doorway. And then through the shimmering air he caught a glimpse of someone approaching him from the road. Two visitors in two days! He half thought—half hoped, even—that it might be the young monk returning, but as the figure came nearer he recognized one of the merchants from a nearby town.

"Abba Anastasius!" called the trader in greeting, respectfully bowing his head before he approached the cell. "Are you able to spare me a few moments of your time?"

"Ammon," the old monk replied, "it's always my honor to welcome you. Come and sit. Let me fetch you water. It's a tiring journey across these sands in the middle of the day."

The merchant climbed down from his donkey, accepting gratefully the monk's cup of water and the accompanying prayer of blessing. Then he pulled a cloth-wrapped package from the donkey's saddlebag. "Someone visited me today offering to sell me something quite unusual," he said handing the package to Anastasius. "It's a Christian relic of some kind. I'd like your opinion on it, abba."

Anastasius gently unwrapped the cloth covering and was not wholly surprised to find himself holding his precious Bible. "It certainly is beautiful," he murmured. "I'd be very glad to own it myself." He ran a finger across the leathery cover. "What price is being asked?"

The merchant named the prodigious sum. Anastasius looked thoughtful, then handed back the book. "It seems a very good price," he said quietly. "I think you should buy it. You've found a real bargain, Ammon." And he said nothing more as the merchant packed the book back into his saddlebag, mounted the donkey and rode away.

Three days later Anastasius was weaving reeds into baskets when he heard a knock at the cell door. He opened it to find the zealous young monk standing before him, clutching a very familiar-looking cloth-wrapped package. Without speaking the young man peered intensely into the older man's eyes. Then finally he burst out, "'A bargain'? Is that all you had to say? 'A very good price'?"

Anastasius nodded, not speaking.

"But that's ridiculous!" cried the young monk. "I *stole* this from you! How could you simply let me get away with that?"

The older monk placed his hand around the younger man's shoulders and guided him back into the cell, where they sat down together. "The abbas tell the story of Abba Serapion, who owned a very fine copy of the Gospels. One day he sold the book and gave all the money he received to the poor. And then he came back to the brothers, grinning, and told them, 'I had a book which told me to sell everything and give the money to the poor. So I sold it!' When I saw you had taken the book, I reminded myself of Serapion. What did I know? Perhaps you needed the book more than I did. Besides, when you came to me, I welcomed you as Christ. I could hardly deny Christ his own book!"

Slowly and thoughtfully the young monk unwrapped and handed back the Bible. "Pray for me, abba," he whispered.

"I've done nothing but pray for you these last three days," replied the old monk.

"Well, it must have done some good," answered the younger man. "After all, you've recovered your book."

Anastasius regarded him for a few moments, then with a smile said, "Oh, I think I've recovered much more than that."

Jesus at the Center

The ancient desert monks understood instinctively what Duns Scotus would later articulate so intellectually: that Jesus is at the very center of Scripture, and any authentic reading of the Bible will ultimately lead to an encounter with Christ. And it is this encounter, this meeting with God on holy ground, that is the very goal and purpose of our reading. To perceive only the text, without perceiving Christ who inhabits the text, is to entirely miss the point. Our ability to meet with Jesus in the pages of Scripture is far more important than any academic mastery of its contents. But the encounter begins with the recognition that the Bible is, first and foremost, a book whose contents are redolent with Christ from first to last.

This simple idea—that Jesus is the center and focus of Scripture—completely transformed the way subsequent generations of Christians read the Bible. In the centuries following the New Testament era the church's greatest thinkers continued to explore and expand the implications of understanding Jesus as the key to interpreting Scripture. In a tradition that can be traced right back to such influential figures as Philo, the gifted first-century Jewish philosopher, and Origen, a remarkable Christian theologian who flourished in Alexandria in the early third century, biblical interpreters came to think of the Bible as consisting of a series of overlapping layers of meaning—layers which combined to form a picture of Christ at the heart of creation.

Before the advent of computer-based technology, animators used to draw cartoons frame by frame on a series of "cels"—transparent celluloid sheets. Every moving element in the picture would be created on a separate cel. For example, one cel might contain a background image of a kitchen. A second would show one of the characters placing cheese into a mousetrap, while on a third the animator would paint a mouse peering around a corner. When the cels were all complete they were overlaid to form a single image: the homeowner baiting the trap while the mouse watched. Each cel makes a certain degree of sense on its own, but only when they are combined do we get the full picture.

In a similar way, these ancient Christian interpreters came to see in Scripture a picture formed from overlapping images, each coherent in itself but only together revealing the whole image. They increasingly came to believe that these layers of meaning not only told the story of the people of God across history, from the creation of the world to the formation of the church, but also spoke throughout—from Genesis to Revelation—of the nature and character of Jesus, of his coming, of our present life in him and of God's eternal desire and intention to reconcile all creation to himself in Christ (2 Cor 5:19).

So what are these overlapping layers of meaning? First, every text of the Bible has a *literal* layer, its straightforward and most obvious sense. This is often very clear, especially in the long sections of biblical narrative; when Scripture says David slew Goliath, or that Jesus was baptized in the Jordan, or when Paul writes that "we have peace with God through our Lord Jesus Christ" (Rom 5:1), the words mean exactly what they say. Not every text is quite so blunt, of course; poetic passages lean heavily on metaphors and imagery that need to be correctly understood and interpreted, and some sections of the Bible are simply obscure and difficult to interpret (the book of Revelation has shipwrecked any number of doomsayers across the ages). But in general the Bible can be read and understood in terms of its plain and obvious meaning, a principle the Protestant Reformers called the "perspicuity of Scripture."

But overlapping that literal layer of Scripture are other deeper layers of meaning. The first of these is usually known as the *allegorical* layer. This is the meaning the text acquires when it is read not simply on its own terms, but in light of the cosmos-shaking events surrounding the life, death and resurrection of Jesus. For example, the book of Exodus tells us that the Israelites passed through the Red Sea, wandered through the wilderness, drank water from the rock Moses struck and ate the bread of heaven. But Paul, as we have seen, relates all this to Christ and his role in delivering the people of Israel: they were baptized in the Red Sea, ate the spiritual food of Christ's body and drank from the rock that is Christ (1 Cor 10:1-5).

In fact, it is Paul who gives us this word *allegorical*. In the fourth chapter of his letter to the Galatians he draws on the Genesis stories about Hagar and Sarah, and writes:

> Now this is an *allegory:* these women are two covenants. One woman, in fact, is Hagar, from Mount Sinai, bearing children for slavery. Now Hagar is Mount Sinai in Arabia and corresponds to the present Jerusalem, for she is in slavery with her children. But the other woman corresponds to the Jerusalem above; she is free, and she is our mother. (Gal 4:24-26, emphasis added)

Paul is not suggesting that the literal sense of these Old Testament stories is untrue. There really was an exodus through the Sea, a wandering in the wilderness and manna from heaven. The two women, Hagar and Sarah, were real flesh-and-blood women. Paul is not purely spiritualizing the texts. But since the advent of Christ he can no longer read them as though they were *only* about a national deliverance, a journey or two feuding wives. He sees in them a deeper significance, another layer of meaning. In every part of Scripture, he sees Christ.

The third layer of meaning is often called the *tropological* layer (from the Greek word *tropos,* meaning a manner or way of life). It is sometimes called the *moral* layer, but that term can be misleading. When we seek to unearth the tropological layer of Scripture we are not primarily looking to define principles of morality and ethics, nor are we looking for the "moral of the story."

Take the tale of David and Goliath in 1 Samuel 17. If we approached that narrative the way we consider one of Aesop's fables, we might try to formulate an appropriate moral to the tale—for example, "strong faith will overcome strong opposition," or "stand firm with God even when the odds are against you." Many contemporary preachers treat the biblical stories in exactly this way, as rich seams from which we can mine practical wisdom—principles to apply and action points to follow through. This may have its place, but has little to do with the layer of meaning we seek here.

Thus, we begin by looking behind the third layer at the second (allegorical) layer of the text: how does this passage relate to Christ? We can see in the conflict between David and Goliath a reflection of the wider cosmic conflict between good and evil, between the kingdom of God and the power of the prince of lies. It doesn't stretch the imagination much to see in David a likeness of Christ, humble and seemingly outmatched by the powers of this world. The defeat of the mighty Goliath is as surprising as Christ's overthrowing of this sinful age through his own death and resurrection. In fact, ancient interpreters found rich soil for an allegorical reading here.

Drawing on this we can explore the tropological layer by asking: how should we live in response to Christ as he is revealed in this passage? The text clearly invites us to align ourselves with Christ in his humility and weakness, rather than adopting the tactics of power and force. In this light the Scripture appears to be calling us to a particular *tropos.* We can read it not only as an encouragement to trust God when we are in a position of weakness but also (like Christ) to deliberately and intentionally embrace weakness and vulnerability for, as Paul reminds us, "whenever I am weak, then I am strong" (2 Cor 12:10). Rather than a simple "moral of the story," this layer of meaning suggests to us ways of living that form a consistent and appropriate response to the reality of Christ in our lives. (We'll begin to explore this in more detail in chapter twelve.)

The final layer is the *anagogical* (from two Greek words meaning "to lead toward"). The question here is: how does this text speak of the way our lives are being drawn into the life of Christ? This has two dimensions. First, the Bible consistently points us toward the consummation of all things in Christ, the "last day" or "end of the age" when God will reconcile all things to himself, when he will usher in his glorious kingdom in all its fullness, and when God will become "all in all" (1 Cor 15:28). Since all history and all human experience is inevitably ordered to that final end, however much we might resist it, we can reasonably expect to find that expectation and hope threaded throughout Scripture. But the Bible also suggests that we are experiencing that "last day" to some degree right now, in the present. God is reconciling all things in Christ, but we are now already reconciled to God. The kingdom is coming, but it is also among us. At the end of the age every knee will bow and every tongue confess that Jesus Christ is Lord (Phil 2:10-11)—but we make that confession on bended knee today. The presence of God, which defines heaven and eternity, is a presence we experience here and now.

The other three layers of Scripture (literal, allegorical and tropological) seek to instill knowledge and faith in us, and elicit a lived response. But this final layer is like the doorway to the throne room itself; it seeks to entice us directly into the living presence of Christ. An ancient (and very compact) Latin rhyme was used to teach the difference between the four layers:

> *Lettera gesta docet,*
> *quid credas allegoria,*
> *moralia quid agas,*
> *quo tendas anagogia.*

Loosely translated, this can be read as:

> *The literal layer teaches us what happened;*
> *the allegorical layer shows where our faith should be placed;*
> *the moral layer tells us how to act in life;*
> *and the anagogical layer reveals what draws us.*

Scripture, then, speaks plainly of the history of God's people, of doctrine and wisdom, of poetry and prophecy. Its deeper layers, though, speak constantly of Christ, the Word of God from eternity. Through these layers of meaning, the Bible provokes us to align our lives in particular ways which are consistent with the way of Christ. And it actively draws us, not only toward our future destiny in Christ, but now, at this present moment, into his immediate presence.

Practicing Christ-Centered Reading

How then might we begin to develop our ability to read the Bible more Christocentrically—that is, as a book that speaks everywhere to us of Christ?

First, it is essential that we develop the skills of attentiveness outlined in chapter ten and have some experience of using those skills in our reading of the Gospels. Until we have learned, at a deep level, to discern and respond to the presence of Christ in the Gospel narratives (where he is most conspicuously present), we will always struggle to identify how, say, Leviticus or Job might be revealing Christ.

Second, we need to approach Scripture with new questions. Typically, many of us are taught to interpret the Bible by asking questions such as: What is the history and context of this passage?

What theology is taught here? Are there principles I need to un-
cover and apply to my life? Are there commands to be obeyed,
promises to treasure or challenges to heed? And all these are, of
course, good and necessary questions. They help us become very
aware of the literal sense of Scripture, the straightforward and
plain meaning of the text—which is by far the most important
layer of meaning. Every other reading of Scripture rests on the
foundation of this literal sense.

But there are other questions we also need to learn to ask. How
does this passage speak of Christ? How does it fit within the
wider sweep of a biblical story centered on Jesus? What does it
reveal about Christ's life, his character and nature, his challenge
and call, his love and grace? How does this text help me frame my
life in appropriate response to the life of Jesus? In what way does
this passage draw me deeper into an experiential relationship
with Christ?

One of the most helpful traditional approaches to reading Scripture, an approach that helps to open up exactly these kinds of
questions, is known as *lectio divina*, or sacred reading. A recovery
of interest in *lectio divina* during recent years has led many Christians and churches to explore a more meditative style of private
and public reading of the Bible. But in my experience *lectio* often
seems to mean little more in practice than "reading the Bible
really slowly, two or three times, with a candle." Genuine *lectio* is
far deeper and richer than this. It is a way of reading that helps to
expose all the different layers of meaning in a passage of Scripture, and at the same time helps us to open every part of the ourselves—senses, imagination, reason, memory, emotions and will—
to God who is present in the biblical text.

The best written description of *lectio divina*, even though it is
some eight centuries old, is *The Ladder of Monks*, a short book written by a medieval French Carthusian prior called Guigo II. At the
beginning of his book Guigo describes the practice of *lectio* in very

simple terms: "One day when I was busy working with my hands I began to think about our spiritual work, and all at once four stages in spiritual exercise came into my mind: reading, meditation, prayer, and contemplation."

Many will be familiar with these four stages by the Latin words Guigo employs: *lectio, meditatio, oratio* and *contemplatio.* Throughout the rest of the book Guigo explains what he means by each of these terms.

Guigo writes that reading, or *lectio* itself, is "the careful study of the Scriptures, concentrating all one's powers on it." It is, he says, "the foundation; it provides the subject matter we must use for meditation." In this first stage of reading we are using perception to the full. We absorb the text as best we can, directing all the power of our senses toward it (throughout most of history Christians have read Scripture aloud, even when reading alone, so that the words are not only seen but also heard—often an enlightening experience, as anyone who has tried it can testify). We also make use of the imagination to allow Scripture to come alive, to speak as fully and presently as possible to us. We try to take everything in; as Guigo expresses it, good reading "puts food whole into the mouth." All this helps us to explore fully the text's *literal* layer of meaning.

Reading is followed by meditation, the act of chewing over the food we have taken in. Meditation, writes Guigo, is "the busy application of the mind to seek with the help of one's own reason for knowledge of hidden truth." This includes analysis and study of the text—considering the language, grammar, context, genre and interpretation—but it also involves the mind in actively seeking the presence of Christ in Scripture. In this way we begin to tease out the *allegorical* layer of meaning. *Meditatio* encourages us to use the skills of cognition, the faculties of memory and reason, to understand the text as fully as possible in the light of our knowledge of the rest of Scripture and of Christ.

This leads us to prayer, *oratio*. But for Guigo the nature of this prayer is very specific: "prayer is the heart's devoted turning to God to drive away evil and obtain what is good." Writing about this drives Guigo to prayer himself:

> So the soul, seeing it cannot attain by itself to that sweetness of knowing and feeling for which it longs, and that the more "the heart abases itself," the more "God is exalted" [see Ps 42:11], humbles itself and betakes itself to prayer, saying: Lord, you are not seen except by the pure of heart. I seek by reading and meditating what is true purity of heart and how it may be had.

This prayer, then, seeks to address the waywardness of our desires and drives—which leads us into the *tropological* layer of meaning. As we meditate on Scripture and find ourselves being drawn nearer to Christ, we become more painfully aware of our corrupted and sinful nature. At this point, our prayer is a longing and begging for grace, for the renewal of our lives, so that we might no longer be alienated from his glorious presence. Prayer addresses our emotions, not only as we feel them but as we inappropriately express them in our habits and behavior.

And finally comes contemplation. "Contemplation is when the mind is in some sort lifted up to God and held above itself, so that it tastes the joys of everlasting sweetness," as Guigo puts it somewhat rapturously. Here we finally settle into the *anagogical* layer of the text. We have carefully absorbed what we have read. We have meditated on it—studied, reflected, pondered, considered. This has led us into a deeper awareness of our fallenness, which has driven us to a desperate prayer for transformation. But in this final step we find ourselves welcomed into the ever gracious presence of Christ, and we experience a longing simply to be allowed to dwell here. This is truly a movement of the heart, a stretching of the soul into God—an act of *intendere*, of intention, reorientation, stretching into the divine. Our whole person is joyfully absorbed into the life of God.

Only Scripture truly has the capacity to be read in this way. Other texts may connect with our souls, but no other quite like this. It is because of this capacity that Christians throughout the ages have spoken of the Bible as inspired, as filled with the breath of God. It is this that leads us to give the Bible our fullest and most intense attention. This book draws us into the living presence of the Creator whose gaze sweeps across the breadth of an unimaginably vast cosmos without losing sight of us, in all our humility and smallness. It is because of the ability of this book to speak to every part of our soul, to touch every facet of our inner life, that we come to it as such ardent seekers and lovers.

Readings

As an introduction to the practice of *lectio divina*, reflect on each of the Old Testament passages below and answer as best as you can these simple questions:

- What does this passage say? How would I summarize it?
- Is there anything in this text that speaks to me of Jesus? Why?
- What does that imply about the way I can live with Christ?
- Does this passage help me draw nearer to Jesus here and now?

Don't forget to record your responses in your notebook or journal. Even if you never go back to read them, just the act of writing them down encourages us to think more clearly. On the whole these readings are somewhat more challenging than those we used last week; the way these Scriptures speak of Christ is less immediately obvious. So don't worry if you find you can't answer every question for every passage; the point is not finding all the answers, but learning the habit of asking the questions.

| Day 1 | Genesis 28:10-17 | (Jacob's vision of the ladder) |
| Day 2 | Exodus 29:1-9 | (the ordination of Aaron) |

Day 3	Deuteronomy 27:1-10	(the inscribed stones of the covenant)
Day 4	Job 3:1-10	(Job laments in his suffering)
Day 5	Jeremiah 20:7-12	(Jeremiah's struggle)
Day 6	Ezekiel 3:22-27	(Ezekiel is held in silence)
Day 7	Jonah 3:6–4:5	(Jonah resents God's mercy)

12

THE DISORDERED SOUL

The living room of Alun's little cottage, nestled in the shadow of the south Wales steelworks, was shrouded in gloom. A haze of cigarette smoke, acridly pungent, hung in the air; the faded yellow curtains were pulled across the windows, veiling the midday sunlight. Alun fussed around over a portable stove in the corner of the room, rustling up tea in a chipped brown pot while I sat in a worn, sagging armchair watching him. His eyes were bloodshot and tired, and a good few days' growth of stubble hung on his cheeks, but Alun was in good humor. He was, for now, sober.

Alun had shown up at our church a few months earlier. He had started appearing at the midweek Eucharist, a short Tuesday morning service with a small but loyal congregation. It was obvious from the beginning that he was testing the waters. He was a large bear of a man whose slurred speech and pickled breath advertised his alcoholism wherever he went. He had recently moved into the area and, looking for friendship, had decided to try the church. Although he was more conspicuous among the dozen or so folks at the Tuesday Eucharist, it also felt a little less public and formal—easier, perhaps, for him to edge in.

The worshipers were elderly, quiet and somewhat conservative, but they were also good Christian people who took the gospel to heart. They embraced Alun. He became a regular fixture at the service—sometimes good and sober, occasionally badly hung over, only once or twice gently inebriated. A couple of members of the congregation took to visiting him at home from time to time. Others would look out for him in the high street, offering a warm greeting or suggesting that he join them for coffee.

I enjoyed visiting Alun. The house was often gloomy and dark; if he was recovering from a bender after falling off the wagon he couldn't bear the bright sunlight. Cigarettes helped reduce the alcohol cravings, so the smell and smoke were a constant feature. But Alun, at his best, was warm, friendly, hospitable and a wealth of fascinating stories. Drinking was his one great vice and flaw, busily destroying an otherwise wonderful man.

And his alcoholism tortured him. As we sat together that lunchtime over tea, he described the battle that raged inside on a daily, hourly, even minute by minute basis. How he longed to break free, to get cleaned up, to find a job, a proper home, to live some kind of normal life—to stop screwing up and destroying himself. But the cravings were so brutal, so severe, so dominating; they gripped his body and shook him, tormented him. He hated living his life from drink to drink but felt powerless to overcome the addiction. His spirit was so, so willing, but the flesh was enslaved.

The apostle Paul understood Alun's problem well. In his letter to the Romans he described Alun's struggle perfectly—and ours too, if we are honest:

> I can will what is right, but I cannot do it. For I do not do the good I want, but the evil I do not want is what I do. . . . I find it to be a law that when I want to do what is good, evil lies close at hand. For I delight in the law of God in my inmost

self, but I see in my members another law at war with the law
of my mind, making me captive to the law of sin that dwells
in my members. (Rom 7:18-19, 21-23)

We are made to be holy, to live well. But our fallenness, the "sin
that clings so closely" (Heb 12:1) has become hardwired into our
bodies. It exerts a seemingly irresistible force over us that constantly drags us away from a life in communion with God. Under
the influence of our disordered drives and desires we constantly
make poor choices and act wrongly; over time those choices
harden into behavioral habits that only serve to ingrain sin more
firmly into our lives. Holiness eludes us.

Created to Love

The opening chapter of the Bible tells us that we are made "in the
image of God" (Gen 1:27). Scholars and theologians have reflected
for over two millennia about exactly what that might mean, but
the apostle John, in his first letter, gives us an important insight
into at least one significant implication. "God is love," he writes,
"and those who abide in love abide in God, and God abides in
them" (1 Jn 4:16). To bear the character of God is to have love
hardwired into our essential nature. The more we are conformed
to the character of God, the more perfectly loving we will become.
We are created to love.

When God calls us to holiness, he roots that call in his own
character: "Be holy," he says to the Israelites, "for I am holy" (Lev
11:44). Holiness, then, cannot simply be an abstract purity of our
interior nature—an unsullied conscience, free from guilt. Rather
it is a summons to pure love, to be the kind of people who can
develop good, deep, loving relationships, both with God and with
other people, relationships that are safe and enriching for all concerned. Jesus certainly seems to understand the call in this way.
In the first half of the Sermon on the Mount he addresses a series

of issues which threaten to undermine the quality of loving relationships: anger, adultery, divorce, deception and revenge. He then
pushes the boundaries of love further than any reasonable morality would seem to demand: "Love your enemies," he says, "and
pray for those who persecute you"; in this way, he says, you will
"be perfect, as your heavenly Father is perfect" (Mt 5:44, 48). Love,
it seems, is the fulfillment of holiness.

Many years later, the great twelfth-century Dominican writer
Thomas Aquinas picked up on this strand of biblical teaching and
made the startling assertion that love was more than the goal of
Christian perfection: it is the fundamental power behind the created order. Just as physicists probe subatomic structure to identify
the basic forces and particles that make up this physical universe,
so Aquinas probed to the depths of Christian theology to identify
the driving energy behind creation itself. In the end, Aquinas argued, everything is grounded in love, since all creation reflects
the character of the one who made it. He suggested that we are not
only made *to* love, we are made *of* love. Everything we do is driven
by this divine quality: all we can do is love.

But Aquinas had no illusions about the terrifying human capacity for sin. He wrote about the lethal power of sin, that "turning away from our last end which is God." He came to see love as
having the kind of awesome power we see in nuclear fusion. Well-
ordered and directed to the right ends, love can transform lives,
inseparably unite people with one another and God, and act as the
harmonious and creative power that holds all creation in being.
But misdirected—allowed to turn in on itself, allowed to run
wildly on the heels of any and every desire of our misguided
hearts—love can become a horrifyingly destructive force, tearing
apart the world from under our feet. Love, rightly ordered, will be
the foundation of the kingdom of God. But grotesquely disordered
love, inordinate self-love, which swirls in on itself like a fierce
tornado, has the capacity to shape tragedies like Auschwitz or the

Rwandan genocide. Sin—love disordered—is horrific. But holiness—love rightly ordered—is life in all its abundance.

Aquinas, in his *Summa Theologica*, discusses the root and origin of sin by comparing two biblical texts, one from the New Testament and the other from the deuterocanonical books. He notes first that Paul writes to Timothy: "the love of money is a root of all kinds of evil" (1 Tim 6:10). But alongside this he sets a line from the apocryphal book of Sirach which says, "pride is the beginning of all sin" (Sir 10:15). Whether or not we want to accept, with Aquinas, the authority of the deuterocanonical text, the point he makes from these verses fits well with the tenor of Scripture as a whole. The first, he says, describes the way in which we allow our hearts to turn to an inappropriate degree toward the beauty and richness of creation. But the second cuts to the deeper and more serious issue of the way we allow our eyes to be turned away from God himself in the first place. As Paul puts it so directly, "they exchanged the truth about God for a lie and worshiped and served the creature rather than the Creator" (Rom 1:25). Our hearts become increasingly holy as they are healed of these twin maladies: our excessive love for creation (fueled by disordered emotional desires), and misdirected love for ourselves (fueled by disordered emotional drives).

Love Misdirected

The most odious corruption of love within our souls takes place when we allow love to become inwardly directed and self-absorbed. Such misdirected love bears fruit in three of the traditional seven "deadly" sins: envy, wrath and pride. We experience envy when we begrudge others their achievements, successes or possessions. Unlike avarice and greed, where we desire those goods for ourselves, envy is more personal and destructive. We are less concerned about securing our own good, and more obsessed with damaging the other person. Unable to value the other person as highly, or even more highly, than ourselves, the only solution when they pull ahead of us in the rat race is to pull them right back again. Envy breeds malice.

Wrath, on the other hand, often springs from frustration with others who seem to be holding us back from our own successes—however trivial those achievements might be. Every day on our roads we see wrath being played out, as drivers compete with one another to be a little faster, a little more cunning, a little better placed to take first place in the flashing river of steel. Who ever got angry when some courteous soul let them change lanes? But when one racer cuts in front of another, sparks will fly—sometimes quite literally, if people lose control of both their anger and their vehicles. When we place ourselves at the center of the universe it is terrifyingly easy to fall prey to rage at those who get in our way. Perhaps it is no accident that the ancient gods were often depicted flinging furious thunderbolts; we made them in our flawed image.

And then there is pride, the all-consuming black hole of the soul. The proud are often beyond envy and wrath (unless they are threatened by another equally as proud); they have already crafted their pedestal and have both feet firmly planted on it. Assured of their own infinite worth and significance they can often appear superficially kind and considerate of others—after all, what do a few polite words cost? But pride incapacitates our ability to love genuinely. The more certain we are of our own importance, our significance and greatness, the less able we are to walk in the footsteps of one who, "though he was in the form of God, did not regard equality with God as something to be exploited, but emptied himself, taking the form of a slave, being born in human likeness" (Phil 2:6-7).

These impulses are disorders of our emotional drives. The emotions that lay behind them are not in themselves wrong or evil—in fact, they are necessary if we are to be able to love well and fully.

The ambition that lies behind envy is what also propels us to undertake monumental creative endeavors, risky business ventures, complex social projects and bold missionary endeavor. Anger, when not distorted into wrath, is the appropriate response demanded by sin, evil and injustice; think of Jesus furiously expelling the merchants from the temple (Jn 2:13-17). And to regard ourselves as creatures of great value and worth is simply to echo the declaration of God at creation: "God saw everything that he had made, and indeed, it was very good" (Gen 1:31). It is when ambition, anger and a sense of personal worth (and other emotional drives such as courage) become disordered that they collapse into envy, wrath and pride; then they are not only unable to help us love God and others, they actively hinder and destroy love.

In the face of this, Christians insist on a simple truth which is strikingly countercultural in our contemporary society, obsessed as it is with self-realization and self-regard: we are not here to love ourselves.

Now that needs some qualification, of course. It is not that we Christians are called to *hate* ourselves. The loathing which some people experience when they look in the mirror is neither natural nor healthy. But contrary to the way many preachers and writers have come to interpret Christ's teaching on the great commandments, the call to "love your neighbor as yourself" (Mt 22:39) does not imply that our first task is to learn self-love. The twelfth-century Cistercian writer Bernard of Clairvaux had a clearer picture. In his short but brilliant work *On Loving God,* he argued that love at its least perfected is inwardly focused, seeking only its own good. And this self-love is not true love at all, merely what happens to the capacity to love when it is corrupted into pride and vanity. As grace begins to reorder our hearts, though, some of that love starts to turn outward, toward God (and our neighbor), drawing us beyond ourselves—even if initially only because of the selfish benefits we can derive from others. A yet more well-ordered heart is able to love God and others for their own sake. And finally, says Bernard, we then truly learn what it means to love ourselves: to be grateful for the gift of ourselves, the only thing we truly have to offer to God and those around us, to express love. Growth in holiness ends in a proper love of self by turning outward to others, not by turning inward on ourselves.

The hallmark of holiness, this constant turning toward others in constant acts of humility and service, is a strikingly obvious characteristic of Jesus. Perhaps the most compelling example occurs on the night of the Last Supper. The apostle John tells us that Jesus, fully aware of his divine origins and significance, was seeking a way to love his disciples "to the end" (Jn 13:1—an equally accurate translation of the Greek could be "to the utmost"). So he stripped off his outer garment and proceeded to perform the work of the lowest, most menial slave: washing the filthy, dirt-crusted feet of those around him. The disciples are shocked and appalled, so much so that Peter is embarrassed for Jesus and tries to refuse. But Jesus persists, teaching them what holiness toward others might mean—and calling them to love one another to exactly the same degree.

Excessive Love

Aquinas, continuing to analyze the effects of sin on the human heart, just as a doctor carefully diagnoses the sick patient, turned from our misdirected drives to our inappropriate desires, the excessive love for creation which is the root of so many kinds of evil. Here is a love that at least looks beyond ourselves, he suggests— but which is nevertheless disordered, since it is not fully turned toward "our last end, which is God." This is love which places the creation above the Creator.

Again, it might help to clarify. The Christian tradition resists the idea that material creation in itself is bad, evil or corrupt. Genesis tells us repeatedly that as God called the various elements of creation into being, he "saw that it was good" (Gen 1:4, 10, 12, 18, 21, 25). As we noted above, human beings delighted him so fully that after their creation he went further, proclaiming the newly formed universe "very good" (Gen 1:31). There are certainly no grounds in Scripture for a religion that delights in the spiritual while denigrating the physical world. The dust from which the sons and daughters of God are made is both very physical and very wonderful.

But it is possible for us to delight in the material creation to an inordinate degree, in ways that are good neither for us, for others or for the wider world—and which certainly draw us away from any depth of intimacy with God. Classically Christians have spoken of three cardinal sins that afflict us in this way: gluttony (an inordinate appetite for food), avarice (an unbalanced desire for wealth), and lust (a disordered love of sexual pleasure).

As with our drives, we need to notice that each of these disordered desires is rooted in an entirely appropriate and necessary emotion. Our appetites for food, material possessions and sexual delight are gifts from God, as are the pleasures which satisfy them. Christian disciplines such as fasting, simplicity and celibacy should not blind us to this essential fact. We do not practice self-denial because food, wealth and sex are somehow intrinsically tainted. Good, orthodox Christian theology celebrates the material world, placing tremendous value on it—which is precisely why acts of self-denial can be an effective sacrificial offering to God. The point of fasting is not that food makes us less pious, but that seeking God with a stronger desire than our appetite for food satisfies a spiritual hunger.

It's fascinating to see the way Jesus engaged with the material world, maintaining a perfectly balanced position: enjoying creation, but not allowing his appetites to take control. Jesus fasted, but he also celebrated at the wedding at Cana, feasted with the

Pharisees and multiplied a handful of loaves to feed a crowd of thousands. He lived in great simplicity yet moved easily among the wealthy and encouraged his disciples to accept the gifts offered by benefactors; we know the disciples kept a purse for making gifts to the poor (a responsibility entrusted to Judas, who was sadly blinded by his avarice). Although he was celibate, Jesus was more willing than most in his culture to be surrounded by (and touched by) women and men, and he clearly had no difficulty forming intimate relationships with people of both sexes—think of the apparent depth of his friendship with both Peter and Mary Magdalene. His emotional desires were always well-ordered and appropriate—and they made it easier, not harder, for him to express love.

Lukewarm Love

The last major barrier to holiness which we face is the cooling of our ardor for God. The Christian tradition has often spoken of this as the spiritual malady of sloth, a translation of the Greek word *akēdia* (sometimes written in its Latinate form, *accidie*). We tend to think of sloth as a very minor issue, little more than oversleeping on a sunny Saturday morning or failing to file our tax returns on time. But for Christians that word has always had a much more pointed meaning: it is the failure to maintain an attentive and passionate love for God, a neglect of the greatest commandment: "love the Lord your God with all your heart, and with all your soul, and with all your mind" (Mt 22:37).

The early desert Christians of Egypt spoke of *akēdia* in vivid and concrete terms as the "noonday demon." Picture the monk in his cell, they would say. As the sun rises, so the monk rises filled with enthusiasm for the new day. Psalms are sung and prayers are recited. The day's work begins. Throughout the morning, the monk remains fervent and attentive to God. But as the burning sun rises high into the sky, time seems to slow. Energy levels drop.

Evening seems so far away, and both work and prayer become unbearably tedious. The monk becomes listless and restless. The pursuit of God comes to an exhausted halt.

This is a beautiful metaphor of the Christian life as a whole, compressed into a single day. Following Christ is a long-haul proposition. It is easy to begin with tremendous enthusiasm, only to find after a number of years that our piety has become a familiar habit and our devotion rote. Church no longer inspires us. Our prayers and Bible readings are dutiful, but not life changing. And at this point it is very easy to allow our white-hot passion for God to cool into a more comfortable glowing ember. This is neither love misdirected nor love to excess. It is love gone cold and dry. It is dangerously easy to let love sleep.

The Cardinal Sins

Aquinas was, of course, drawing heavily on the ancient Christian tradition of the seven "deadly" sins: envy, wrath, pride, gluttony, avarice, lust and sloth. Theologians more commonly call them the "cardinal" sins; the Latin word *cardinalis* was used to describe the hinge on a door. And that is the character of these seven vices; they are not some arbitrary collection of sins pulled from the whole range of human behavior—they are the "hinge" sins which open the door to every other distortion of love in our lives.

Envy, wrath and pride are misdirected love. Gluttony, avarice and lust are excessive love. Sloth is lukewarm love. But despite all that, they are still love. Horrifically distorted, repulsively corrupted love—but yet love. Because in the end evil cannot overcome what God has made, and it cannot produce anything new. It depraves, it distorts, it demeans. But it cannot *destroy*, and it cannot *create*.

And what has become defaced and diseased can be cleansed and healed. Although the image of God within us—the capacity to love as God loves—has been disfigured by sin, it can never be entirely

erased. And God, by grace, is restoring that loving nature in each
of us whose lives are hidden in Christ. As the apostle John writes,
"Beloved, we are God's children now; what we will be has not yet
been revealed. What we do know is this: when he is revealed, *we
will be like him*, for we will see him as he is" (1 Jn 3:2, emphasis
added). Within us fallen people, love has been corrupted. But
within us redeemed people, love is being made whole.

Readings

Each of this week's readings gives us the opportunity to reflect on
love: the loving character of God, our call to live as those made in
the image of God, and the effect of sin as it distorts love within us.

As you read, pray, meditate and journal on these readings allow
yourself to be drawn beyond simple analysis of the text and its
ideas (although this is the crucial first step in our reading). Thomas
à Kempis once wrote, "I would rather feel contrition than define
the word." Similarly, it is more important for us to be able to enter
into and experience the loving nature of God—and the image of
God within us, both in its corrupted state and as God is healing
it—than to be able to explain it.

Day 1	1 John 4:7-12	(God's character is love)
Day 2	Matthew 5:38-48	(the call to love)
Day 3	Matthew 5:17-20	(Jesus fulfills the law of love)
Day 4	Matthew 22:34-40	(the greatest commandment)
Day 5	Romans 6:1-11	(dead to sin, alive to God)
Day 6	Galatians 5:16-26	(the fruit of the Spirit)
Day 7	1 Corinthians 13:1-13	(the greatest gift is love)

13

A LIFE DESIRED

❧

Being "holy" doesn't seem very desirable to many people in our contemporary society. Those who speak up for virtue are often derided as moralistic, sanctimonious or holier-than-thou. The media reacts sharply against "preachy" public figures who presume to tell us how to order our private lives. And those who appear to be living lives of moral rectitude are treated with suspicion: can they really be so pure? Or are they hiding darker truths about themselves—clean on the outside but as filthy as the rest within? We have seen so many spectacular falls from grace among our celebrities, politicians and church leaders that we have become wary of taking virtue at face value. There are, it would seem, more wolves in sheep's clothing than there are genuine sheep.

And who, after all, wants the sheep's life anyway? Frankly, to many of us sin just seems a lot more fun than sainthood. Just as the devil sometimes seems to have all the best music, so he often appears to have all the best and most entertaining pursuits, leaving the pious to their hair shirts and homilies. It often looks as though the good and the godly are gingerly picking their way through a tightly fenced minefield of "thou shalt nots" while sinners romp in wide open meadows. Holiness only holds us back.

Or so it appears. But these images of sanctity and sin fall apart when we take a closer look at them. In fact, as we take the time to reflect on the nature of virtue and vice, we make the unexpected discovery that, while sin acts like a malignant cancer slowly tearing us apart from within, it is holiness that leads us into the fullest, most enriching experience of life. We are made to be holy. We just don't always understand exactly what holiness is.

The English word *holiness* is derived from the Anglo-Saxon word *hal*, from which we inherit words like "hale" and "health"; the root idea the word expresses is integration, completion or (and this word also comes from the same English root) wholeness. The wholeness God desires for us happens as the various desires and disorders of our souls are healed and united toward a single end: love. As God's grace draws us into an ever fuller life of sacrificial, self-giving love, we increasingly become the people we were created to be, people who fully reflect the essential character of God. Perfect holiness is perfect love, and this is the goal toward which Jesus continually beckons us, no matter how frequently we fall short. As we live into the way of Christ, our twisted self-love is slowly straightened out, our excessive love for creation is brought into appropriate proportion and our lukewarm love for God is kindled into burning fire. As we grow in virtue we develop integrity, an integration of our scattered souls into one unified whole.

The Joy of Holiness

The surprising discovery made by those who pursue this integrity and healing of spirit is that holiness brings such tremendous *pleasure*. We are often seduced by the cultural assumption that sin is fun and saintliness is dreary (although necessary). Nothing could be further from the truth. Of course, at the moment of indulgence sin can be tremendously enjoyable. It's often that spike of pleasure that draws people back for more overindulgence, illicit sex, angry outbursts, venomous backbiting or shameless self-promotion.

But it's all too easy to forget that we commit these acts within a universe that has a clear moral structure. And when we push against the grain of the universe, the universe has a tendency to push back. We're painfully familiar with this in the physical world. If I ignore the fact that the universe is structured to include gravity, I can leap off a tall building and experience the immediate euphoria of unassisted flight. My rapid downward acceleration will be rewarded with a burst of adrenaline and a heightened sense of awareness. All of which might seem tremendously enjoyable until the moment the universe pushes back—in this case, rather forcefully. The first few seconds of flight may be fantastic, but a few seconds after landing I'm likely to have formed a serious regret that I made that leap.

Likewise, the moral structure of the universe pushes back at us. Anyone who has ever overindulged with beer knows just how this feels. At the time, the experience is marvelous; drink enough beer and all your problems will float away. All your inhibitions will melt, and you'll laugh, sing and dance the night away. Your excessive behavior will be rewarded with an excess of pleasure, and who could complain about that? But the next morning the moral structure of the universe pushes back—and how. That blinding headache, that swirling nausea in the pit of your stomach, that longing to close the curtains, curl up in bed and simply die: that is the moral universe knocking hard at your door.

Misdirect your love inward, into envy, wrath and pride, and the consequences will haunt you: alienation from others, mockery, distrust, hatred and loneliness. Allow your love for physical creation to run amok and you'll suffer the results: obesity, disease, ill health, corruption and ultimately dissatisfaction. Let the fire of love for God burn down and extinguish itself and you'll backslide through spiritual lethargy and torpor to disengagement, and fi-

nally perhaps lose your faith in God altogether (a painful experience, as too many have borne witness).

But well-ordered love, genuine holiness that orders our lives
toward others and toward God and knows how to hold all created
things in careful balance, this love runs right along the grain of
the moral universe. Those who learn their true value in God's
sight learn also the value of others and can rejoice in their successes and achievements without malice. Those who nurture a
balanced enjoyment of creation enjoy pleasure without the sting
of overindulgence. Those who burn with love for God are often
surprised to find that their joy in life *increases* exponentially. As
Paul wrote, "There is no law against such things" (Gal 5:23). C. S.
Lewis once wrote: "We are half-hearted creatures, fooling about
with drink and sex and ambition when infinite joy is offered us."
He knew the secret: sinners may have the wildest parties, but
saints have the most fun.

Desiring Virtue

How, then, can our reading of Scripture lead us more fully into a
Christlike life of virtue, a life in which divine love is expressed as
openly as possible without being misdirected or stunted?

Guigo II, the twelfth-century Carthusian abbot we first encountered in chapter eleven, has an interesting and helpful perspective on this question. The Carthusians may be the most as-
cetic monastic order in the Western world. Philip Gröning's 2007
movie *Into Great Silence* presented a view of contemporary life in
the Grande Chartreuse, the mother house of the Carthusian order.
The three-hour documentary was slow and reflective, but also fascinating; it was like looking back in time into the world of an
austere medieval community. The monks live in such startling
simplicity they make the Amish look decadent. Deep in the French
Alps, far from the technology and hurry of modern society, they
follow a carefully measured routine of prayer, silence, meditation

and heavy labor, which has stood largely unchanged for centuries. Gröning was only permitted to film in the monastery on the condition that he came alone, with a minimum of equipment and presented his record without commentary or music; it was to be a plain and simple presentation of a plain and simple way of life. These folks take the pursuit of God and virtue deeply seriously.

We might expect, then, that Guigo would commend to us the careful study of the Bible's moral and ethical precepts, and an intense effort to frame our lives deliberately around them. In fact, his approach was quite different. Living in a community which has intentionally stripped life down to its bare essentials, Guigo had plenty of opportunity to come to know himself very clearly; there are no distractions to hide from yourself behind in a Carthusian house. He knew very well the darkness of his own heart, his inability to love God and others with all his heart, soul and mind. He also recognized his moral limitations, the impossibility of engaging in some kind of ethical self-help program to pull himself into virtuous living by his own bootstraps.

Guigo faced an important truth that many of us choose to avoid: God intended that we be moral creatures in a moral universe, but we have squandered virtue and are incapable of recreating it. What virtue we now have, and what virtue we may come to have, is all of grace. Virtue is a gift. To pretend otherwise is to lack self-awareness at a fundamental level.

Guigo invites us to come to Scripture not in order to define the principles of virtue so we can put them into practice but so that our appetite for virtue, our desire for goodness, can be kindled and fanned into flame. As we draw nearer to Christ in Scripture we become more deeply aware of our own brokenness and fallen nature. We recognize that the wholeness of life we see in Christ is not echoed in our own character. And this awakens in us a longing for transformation and renewal, a yearning to become more Christlike. That longing finds expression in the sighs and groans of our prayer. "The soul," writes Guigo, "seeing that it cannot attain by itself to that sweetness of knowing and feeling for which it longs . . . betakes itself to prayer." And that is exactly where we need to find ourselves. On our knees, arms outstretched to God and humbled by our inadequacies and failures, we are entirely ready to receive as much grace as humanly possible. We are open to God.

Rivers of Grace

The simple act of reading Scripture, by itself, cannot reverse the degradation of the soul, the corruption of our drives and desires. It cannot heal our damaged souls and make us more holy. Although the Bible can show us what a well-ordered, integrated and life-giving individual or society looks like, this knowledge alone is not enough to enable us to become such people or communities. Whatever spiritual healing we experience in this life is a result of the pure and direct grace of God at work within us; it is Christ who heals, not the pages of a book.

But prayerful engagement with the Bible has an essential part to play in the healing process. It is by grace we are healed, and our reading of Scripture does help us become increasingly open to welcoming and receiving that grace. The first page of the Psalter illustrates the idea vividly:

Happy are those . . .
[whose] delight is in the law of the LORD,
    and on his law they meditate day and night.
They are like trees
    planted by streams of water,
which yield their fruit in its season,
    and their leaves do not wither. (Ps 1:1-3)

The imagery is beautiful and striking. In the psalm, the poet describes the fate of two plants, one rooted beside cool and refreshing waters, and the other thirsting in dry, sandy soil, blown by the desert winds. The well-watered tree drives down strong, firm roots and flourishes. As it draws in the life-giving water, it puts forth leaves and fruit; its life is so abundant and overflowing it is able to sustain and refresh even those who pass by with its harvest.

The desert plant, by contrast, grows far from water. It becomes dry and brittle, struggling to hang on in its harsh environment. Its branches are barren—no leaves, no fruit, nothing to offer the world. As the scorching sun saps the last of its strength its roots wither; the parched, dusty sirocco pries it from the ground and carries it into oblivion: "like chaff that the wind drives away" (v. 4).

Here, says the psalmist, is the contrast between two ways of living. One is a life fully open to grace, to God, to the life of the Spirit. The other is closed, resisting God and turned inward to draw on its own meager resources. One tends to result in virtue, and the other in sin. But the contrast is not between the *saint* and the *sinner*. The picture here is more akin to Jesus' parable about the Pharisee and the tax collector (Lk 18:9-14). The Pharisee is so confident of his own ability to live a good and virtuous life he boasts before God. But the tax collector knows his own weakness and brokenness; he hides his face from God and begs for grace. The Pharisee seems to have cornered the market in holiness, but in truth his life is in mortal danger. He is living in the wilderness of his own dry soul. But the tax collector, who has abandoned all pretense of holiness, thrusts his roots desperately into the river of grace and drinks in God. And it is this man, not the Pharisee, who will flourish.

The psalmist paints a picture of someone choosing deliberately, intentionally, time and again, to place him- or herself before God's presence through meditation on God's Word. But as we ourselves reflect on the psalm as a whole, it becomes very clear what this

particular meditation does *not* involve. It is not Bible study or exegesis. It is not the creation of an ethical system. It is not the elu-
cidation of moral principles to be put into action. The person described in the psalm is sufficiently self-aware to recognize his or
her own moral bankruptcy, the inability to renew the soul solely
through the soul's own resources. Instead, the psalmist describes
someone who simply seeks to become immersed in the spacious
and glorious universe of Scripture, seeking the life-giving and
healing presence of God.

Richard Foster, calling this the spiritual art of "indirection,"
writes:

> We cannot by direct effort make ourselves into the kind of
> people who live fully alive to God. Only God can accomplish
> this in us. . . . Spiritual disciplines [like meditation on Scrip-
> ture] in and of themselves have no merit whatsoever. . . .
> Their purpose—their only purpose—is to place us before
> God. Then the grace of God steps in, takes this simple offer-
> ing of ourselves, and creates out of it the kind of person who
> embodies the goodness of God.

Those who meditate on Scripture become like a fruit-bearing tree
planted beside refreshing waters, able to draw constantly from the
cool, fresh streams of grace. And just as for the tree the result is
green shoots bursting forth and succulent fruit growing, so these
people find themselves naturally—without any direct and deliberate effort—bearing the Spirit's virtuous fruit: "love, joy, peace, pa-
tience, kindness, generosity, faithfulness, gentleness, and self-
control" (Gal 5:22-23). As the grace of God washes over them, a
healing of the soul begins.

Paul well knew that we are largely unable to resist the power of
sin in our lives; its destructive force is all but overwhelming. But
sin, in turn, is unable to resist the transforming power of God's
grace. If we are to grow in holiness, to become increasingly Christ-

like in our character and behavior, we would be wise to invest less energy in trying to wrestle down the dragon within and spend more time soaking in the irresistible presence of God. And as the psalmist understood, one of the best ways we can do that is by "meditating day and night" on Scripture.

Readings

Seeking to humble ourselves before God rather than seeking to reform ourselves using our own meager resources doesn't mean, of course, that we simply stop trying to live a good, ethical life and abandon ourselves to sin until God chooses to reshape us. We don't abdicate our moral responsibilities; we still need to "pursue righteousness, faith, love, and peace" (2 Tim 2:22). But we do recognize that genuine transformation into Christlikeness is an act of sheer grace, a renewing gift of the Holy Spirit. Our reading of Scripture should reflect that understanding.

The passages below all speak, in one way or another, about the life of virtue. They extol the benefits of holiness, describe its nature and encourage us to pursue it. Over the coming days you might want to spend some time immersed in these passages, letting your roots sink into their refreshing water. But resist the temptation to engage them as entry requirements for the kingdom of God. However poorly you match up to this biblical picture, you know that you are saved—brought into relationship with God through Christ—by grace, not by your good works. If you fall far short of the holiness Scripture describes, don't despair: you cannot fall out of reach of the love of God. Similarly, however well you think you could fulfill all these conditions if they were God's entry requirements, don't be deceived. You cannot become truly Christlike under your own steam, and any attempt to do so will result in frustration at best and a spectacular and painful fall at worst.

Instead, use these passages to whet your appetite for virtue.

Allow them stimulate your heart and soul with a longing desire to live a life more closely aligned to that of Jesus. Let yourself be driven to your knees by your yearning for holiness. Open yourself as fully as possible to the Spirit's gentle work in your heart and life. Of course, you may sense that God is leading you to some practical action that will help nurture virtue—an act of service, for example, or a period of fasting. Be attentive and obedient to such leadings. But always return to this prayer of desire and longing.

Day 1	Deuteronomy 30:11-20	(Choose life)
Day 2	James 4:1-10	(humble yourself before God)
Day 3	1 Peter 5:1-11	(humble yourselves before one another)
Day 4	Romans 12:9-21	(overcome evil with good)
Day 5	Ephesians 5:3-20	(Be careful how you live)
Day 6	1 Thessalonians 4:1-12	(a life pleasing to God)
Day 7	Hebrews 13:1-6	(living well in community)

14

BEYOND THE BIBLE

Toward the beginning of a course on world religions at the theological college where I trained for ministry, our lecturer had startled us by saying, "I don't really want to teach you about Islam or Buddhism or Judaism. You see, the problem is that these religions don't really exist."

He paused for a moment while we looked back at him, confused and uncertain. Religions don't exist? That seemed an unlikely proposition. After all, centuries of history, thousands of churches, temples and mosques around the world, strong and rich philosophical and cultural traditions that had shaped the way we all live—all these would appear to suggest otherwise. Across the room I could see one of the students sitting with pen poised over his notebook wondering: should I write this down?

The lecturer could clearly sense our consternation. "Think about it," he continued. "Where can you find Hinduism? When has Buddhism ever walked down the street toward you? Have you ever met Judaism? Ever shaken hands with Christianity? Ever eaten a meal with Islam?" He put down his notes and stretched out his hands expressively. "A religion is a really big idea, a philosophy, a huge and tremendously complex way of thinking," he said. "But that's all—it's not real, not like people and chairs and dogs are real." He looked intently around the room. "You'll never meet a religion. But you'll meet hundreds of religious *people*. I'm not interested in whether or not you understand religion; I want to know that you understand people. Not just what they believe, but *who they are*."

And so we began a fascinating journey exploring not the great world belief systems but the lives and experiences of those who professed them. A journey which led a group of us, one damp gray afternoon, to an unassuming red brick building on the corner of a suburban street in southwest England. On the outside the building looked like another drab suite of offices tacked on the end of a row of houses. But everything changed once we stepped over the threshold. Suddenly our noses were filled with the fragrance of exotic spices. The place was awash with bright color: walls painted in bright blues and saffron; yellow cloth draped over tables; gaudy framed pictures hung on every surface. The contrast with the quiet English street outside was striking; this was a taste of the East. We had entered one of Bristol's Sikh Gurdwaras.

We were warmly welcomed by a handful of smiling, turbaned men who briefly introduced themselves and offered to sit with us during the service which was about to take place. They led us into the Darbar, the main hall of the Gurdwara. Dozens of people were scattered around the hall, sitting cross-legged and talking quietly with one another. At the front of the room a huge tasseled canopy hung from the ceiling, embroidered white silk with a luxurious golden fringe. Beneath the canopy, on a low table, rested one of the largest books I have ever seen in my life; it was three or four feet tall, and laid open its pages reached almost as far as a man's arms might stretch. Both open pages were lettered with the elegant, flowing Gurmukhi script, the text surrounded by a colorful illuminated border. Behind the book sat an immaculately dressed Sikh man waving a *chaur,* a kind of horsehair fan, looking for all the world like the servant of an oriental potentate. Our Sikh hosts, on entering, immediately removed their shoes and bowed respectfully.

This book was the *Guru Granth Sahib*, the Sikh holy book. According to Sikh tradition there were a series of ten gurus from the sixteenth century onward who laid the foundations of Sikh faith and practice. The first was known as Guru Nanak Dev; he was held in such esteem by those who followed after him that they each took his name, Nanak, as their own; Sikh's sometimes speak of the "spirit of Nanak" being passed from one guru to the next. Over the years their teachings were collected into a single great tome, a written record of the words of the gurus. The ninth guru, Guru Gobind Singh, proclaimed toward the end of his life that this book was henceforth to be regarded as the last and eternal guru, the repository of the "spirit of Nanak" and the guide for all Sikhs to come. The book itself was elevated to the status of Guru, and plays a central role in the life and worship of all Sikh communities.

Sikhs treat *Guru Granth Sahib* as a living person: the embodiment of the life of the past gurus. They believe that, although the book is not God, it does in some way incarnate the divine spirit, which is why it is accorded such veneration and respect. Wherever the book is present, there the gurus are also present. When a copy of the *Guru Granth Sahib* is damaged beyond repair, it is not simply thrown out: in a ceremony known as *agan bhet* it is ceremonially cremated and mourned. Clearly, for Sikhs, this is no ordinary book.

An Extraordinary Book

For Christians, too, the Bible is no ordinary book. As we have seen, it pulses with the Spirit of God. Through this book we can be drawn into the presence of God who breathes life into its pages.

The voice of God speaks through Scripture, offering a word that is "living and active, sharper than any two-edged sword, piercing until it divides soul from spirit, joints from marrow; it is able to judge the thoughts and intentions of the heart" (Heb 4:12). During her coronation service in 1953 Queen Elizabeth II was presented with a copy of the Bible by the moderator of the General Assembly of the Church of Scotland; as he handed her the book he said: "Our gracious Queen: to keep your Majesty ever mindful of the law and the Gospel of God as the Rule for the whole life and government of Christian Princes, we present you with this Book, the most valuable thing that this world affords. Here is Wisdom; This is the royal Law; These are the lively Oracles of God." Christians throughout the centuries would be happy to echo the sentiment.

But the Bible is not God, and the danger of elevating Scripture beyond its proper place is always present. We are not given the Bible so we can be led deeper into the Bible: Scripture seeks always to lead us deeper into God. We are not called to be obedient to the Bible, but to God who speaks through the Bible. We are not a Bible-centered people; we are a Christ-centered people. Our lives are shaped by Scripture, but not lived for Scripture; to paraphrase Christ, we might affirm that the Bible was given for the benefit of people, not people for the Bible. We are, perhaps, a little too eager to proclaim ourselves "Bible-believing Christians." We are not. We are God-believing, Christ-centered, Spirit-empowered Christians whose faith is formed and fortified by the Bible. The difference is more than just words.

There is a famous icon of the Trinity which was painted by the Russian iconographer Andrei Rublev in the early fifteenth century. The icon, based on the narrative in Genesis which describes Abraham being visited by three angels (Gen 18:1-15), shows three figures seated around a table: God the Father, Jesus and the Holy Spirit. The different figures are gesturing toward one another; Jesus is quietly pointing to the Spirit, while the Spirit is

directing our gaze toward the
Father. The Father is turned outward toward us, as we contem-
plate the icon, as though inviting
us to be drawn into this mysterious trinitarian community; there
is even an open space at the table,
facing toward us. In various ways
each of these three is redirecting
our attention to lead us deeper
into the divine life.

In just the same way the Bible
leads us beyond the Bible. Scrip-
ture is noticeably lacking in self-reflection: there are very few pas-

Rublev's icon of the Trinity

sages of the Bible that discuss the nature of the Bible itself. The
text never seeks to draw us deeper into itself but always points
away toward the divine Author. Simply reading the Bible is never
our final goal; it is always a means to the greater end of participation in life with God. Just as in Revelation John notes that in the
new heavenly Jerusalem "I saw no temple in the city, for its temple
is the Lord God the Almighty and the Lamb" (Rev 21:22), we might
also ask whether we will still be reading Scripture when the kingdom of God is revealed in its fullness. When we are in the eternal,
unmediated presence of God, what need will we have for these
written words?

From Reading to Contemplation

All good reading of Scripture inevitably leads, then, to contemplation. This comes as a surprise to many of us nurtured in more
evangelical traditions who have long been encouraged to ground
our reading of the Bible in action, in application of principles discovered, in practicing whatever we find taught in Scripture. And
of course this is vitally important, as we saw in chapter thirteen.

But this should never be the end point of our reading. If we allow the "living out" of Scripture to become the final stop in our reading of the Bible, we have largely missed the point; the real goal is "living into" Scripture, dwelling patiently within these pages until we are drawn through them into the life of God himself. This call to presence is a call to contemplation.

Christians in the contemporary Western church often struggle to understand and appreciate the vital importance of contemplation. We have convinced ourselves that our call, our purpose, and our mission lie essentially in *activity*. We who follow Christ are, we are sure, summoned to change the world. Some folks are fond of quoting these words of Teresa of Ávila, the great sixteenth-century writer on the spiritual life:

> Christ has no body now but yours;
> no hands, no feet on earth but yours.
> Yours are the eyes through which He looks compassion on
>   this world.
> Christ has no body now on earth but yours.

In fact, Teresa never wrote anything of the sort and would almost certainly have found the sentiment shocking. The poem appears nowhere in her collected works or letters. It would be surprising if it did; as a key figure in the Counter Reformation movement within the Roman Catholic church of her day, steeped in a theology of the Eucharist that spoke boldly of the literal transformation of the bread and wine into the actual body and blood of Jesus, she would hardly be likely to pen the words, "Christ has no body now but yours." But more than this, the little poem also directly undermines the foundations of the contemplative life itself to which Teresa and those around her were so passionately committed—a fact we perhaps find hard to appreciate, because we have become so wildly activist and so alienated from our Christian contemplative heritage.

It might help us shift our perspective a little if we ask ourselves a simple question: Why does God need us? We can clarify the question by asking it in a variety of different contexts. What aspect of the kingdom of heaven is God unable to implement without our assistance? Which injustices is he incapable of correcting alone? Who are the people he is powerless to bring to saving faith without our intervention? How do we play an indispensable role in the redemption of all creation in Christ?

If we stop for even a moment to think about it, of course, we know that these are absolutely nonsensical questions. The kingdom of God is coming and is already breaking through around us. God is restoring all things to himself in Christ. The day of the Lord, which comes like a thief in the night or like lightning flashing across the sky, approaches—whether we like it or not. There is nothing we can do either to postpone or hasten that day; only the Father knows the day and the hour. However hard we try to resist or welcome the kingdom, it comes in whatever way God graciously wills. It is, after all, his kingdom, not ours. And he is perfectly capable of bringing redemption, salvation, freedom, justice, liberation and a new heaven and earth—without any help from us.

We know this. But so much of our activism proclaims the opposite. We must proclaim the gospel, we say—or people will die and fall into the burning pit of hell! As though God's will from before all time that someone should find life in Christ could be frustrated by our indolence. As though we had forgotten that Jesus said, "Not one [sparrow] will fall to the ground apart from your Father" (Mt 10:29). We must campaign for justice, we say—or people will be left perpetually in their suffering, their marginalization, their distress. As though God no longer hears the cry of his people, or is impotent or unwilling to act, or has closed his heart to the poor and friendless. Our activity is propelled by the implicit idea that God's great design for the universe will somehow fail without our heroic efforts. We become a driven people.

The very basis of the contemplative life is the realization that the exact opposite is true. Contemplative prayer is only possible if we accept and believe in the most fundamental way that in Christ (not in us) "the kingdom of God has come near" (Mk 1:15). If it were true that the coming of the kingdom, whether in mission or in works of peace and justice, depended so greatly on us, what possible excuse could there be for indulging in the luxuries of silence, solitude and prayer? Would it not be a dereliction of our calling to abandon our activity in a needy world in order to satisfy our own desires for inner peace? How could withdrawing into the silence and obscurity of some monastery, hermitage or retreat possibly be of any value to the church or the world? Isn't it spiritual selfishness? This is exactly how the contemplative life is so often portrayed in the contemporary world; the tragedy is that the church too often echoes the complaint.

But in reality contemplation is an act of profound trust. Trust that God is able to run the universe without our constant intervention. Trust that God's love and purposes for creation cannot and will not be frustrated by human resistance. And trust that the time we take seeking to dwell in the presence of God is time invested with eternal value, not time fruitlessly wasted—a reflection of the way time will be experienced when the kingdom comes in all its fullness. This is the trust described in Julian of Norwich's famous vision of the hazelnut. The fourteenth-century English nun lived during an extraordinarily tumultuous time in history: the ebbing and flowing of the Hundred Years' War left people living under the constant shadow of violence, while the Black Death swept in ravaging waves across Europe, killing up to a third of the population. In the midst of this Julian experienced a vision in which she saw a small ball, the size of a hazelnut, resting in the palm of God's hand. She was told that this tiny ball was all creation, the unimaginable entirety of the universe. She was astounded; it seemed so fragile and delicate, as though it could all be swept away in a moment. But a voice reassured her: "It lasts and always will, because God loves it; and thus everything has being through the love of God." For Julian, it was trusting in this which made prayer possible.

An Uncomfortable Invitation

The Bible draws us into this contemplative experience. But for many of us such prayer is strange and unfamiliar. We feel comfortable with praise, adoration, intercession, conversation—those word-filled forms of prayer in which we are always active, always speaking, always expressing ourselves to God. The great prayer of silence, though, fills us with uncertainty. What will happen? What if nothing happens? More worryingly, what if *something* happens? Will God speak? What will he say? And what if he doesn't speak— what do I do then?

Traveling through an airport in one of the southeastern states recently, I was asked to step aside at security; something unusual had shown up in my hand luggage on the x-ray. I knew right away what it was: a small glass ornament I'd been given following a speaking engagement a couple of days earlier. But the TSA agent explained, with typical Southern grace and politeness, that he had a protocol to follow and the bag had to be searched. It was a slow day at the airport and I had plenty of time before my flight, so I wasn't worried. We chatted amiably as he unpacked the bag.

After a few moments he drew a small blue book from the bag and looked at it with interest. It was a copy of Martin Laird's *Into the Silent Land*, one of the best books on contemplative prayer I've ever had the pleasure to read. I'd already worked through it a number of times and was using the opportunity of a series of flights within a few days to spend time with it again. The agent read the subtitle of the book aloud: *The Practice of Contemplation*.

"Looks like an interesting book," he said, turning it over to

peruse the back cover. I agreed. He put down the book and continued searching the bag; then he paused again and looked up at me.
"Not many people do that any more—contemplation, I mean.
They don't make the time. No appetite for it. I guess they don't
want to face the most important question we can ask."

"What do you think that is?" I asked him, surprised (I hadn't
turned up at airport security expecting a conversation quite like
this one).

"The most important question?" he replied. *"Who am I?"* There
was a moment's silence, and then he pushed the bag across the
table toward me. "Thank you, sir," he said. "You can go." I walked
away with my head spinning.

All my experience teaching prayer to others tells me that the
TSA agent was right: often the idea of an open-ended, uncontrol-
lable exposure to the presence of God makes us very uncomfortable. It should. In contemplative prayer we place ourselves without reservation in the hands of a God vast beyond our imagining,
more powerful than we could ever hope to express, and fiercely
holy. Any sane person who prays in this way, in the full knowledge
of what they are doing, would be right to feel apprehensive. After
all, God is not tame or predictable. He will not bend his will to
ours or submit to our direction or control. But he is so good, so
gracious and so gentle; his love for us is beyond measure or description. We approach him with respect, with awe, with reverence—but not with fear.

And oh, how he longs for us to draw near.

Readings

This week's readings have one simple aim: to provoke your desire
to dwell in Christ's presence.

Throughout the course of this book, we have constantly engaged with Scripture as a place where God can be encountered

and Christ may be known. We have explored a variety of approaches to reading the Bible that can make us more attentive, more alert and more aware of that presence. We have explored ways of praying with Scripture that engage every aspect of our being, making us more present to God.

But in the end, the real trick is learning to dwell with God. Simply to remain before him, enjoying his company, allowing him to delight in you and heal you through his grace. Let these readings touch your heart, orient your will toward God, and entice you to come before his face.

Then stay there.

Day 1	Psalm 63:1-8	(desire for the living God)
Day 2	Psalm 123	(the soul looking to God)
Day 3	Psalm 131	(the soul resting in God)
Day 4	Luke 10:38-42	(sitting at the feet of Jesus)
Day 5	John 15:1-9	(abiding in Jesus)
Day 6	Revelation 1:12-16	(a vision of Jesus)
Day 7	Revelation 7:9–8:1	(the worship—and silence— in heaven)

15

FRIENDSHIP WITH JESUS

Contemplative reading of the Bible is the art of dwelling in the presence of our limitless God within the rich, complex, immense and beautiful universe of Scripture. It's not simply that we stop talking, stop listening or stop doing *anything*. Contemplation is more a shift of perspective: rather than focusing on our prayer, our meditations, our reflections or even on what we hope God might say or do, we allow our focus to settle on God himself, and we allow ourselves to rest attentively before him. The psalmist captures the idea marvelously:

> O Lord, my heart is not lifted up,
>   my eyes are not raised too high;
> I do not occupy myself with things
>   too great and too marvelous for me.
> But I have calmed and quieted my soul,
>   like a weaned child with its mother;
>   my soul is like the weaned child that is with me.
>   (Ps 131:1-2)

We often come to God like babes who are not yet weaned, clamoring for gifts and attention. "O Lord, listen to me! Hear my prayers! Do this, do that, give us the other! What should I do about this situation, this person, this problem? What is your purpose for my life? Would you bless me, heal me, touch me, renew me, enrich me?" But the weaned child has ceased all this pestering. It has learned to be confident that nourishment and care will be provided; it is able to rest in its mother's love. All it desires is to be in the presence of the mother, to be held in her arms, to hear the beating of her heart.

Contemplative prayer is the soul similarly at rest in our Father's arms, listening to his heartbeat, rejoicing in his loving presence. It is no more complex or arcane than this.

Of course, this doesn't mean that other forms of prayer are somehow inferior, the prayer of lesser Christians who have not yet achieved some kind of spiritual maturity. There is always a place for voicing our worship, the praises of God; always a need to pray for others; always a time and place for lamenting and weeping before God, seeking his intervention. Contemplative prayer doesn't supplant other forms of prayer, it completes them.

Imagine a married couple sitting together and talking over the dinner table. The conversation ranges widely. She tells him about a funny experience from that morning. He reminds her of a commitment they have made for later in the week. She talks about a book she has been reading, and how it has affected her. He asks if she's heard from a friend who has been ill. And so the conversation meanders along as they share their lives—being thankful, expressing concerns, passing along news. In many ways, much of our prayer is like this, a conversation with God in which we express our delights and concerns, and listen for his response, his guidance, his reassurance.

Now picture the scene an hour later. The dinner table has been cleared and the summer sun is setting outside. He suggests that they sit out on the porch swing to watch the sun go down. They pour two glasses of chilled lemonade, step outside and sit together enjoying the warm evening. What now do they talk about? It hardly matters. Perhaps they simply sit in companionable silence while the day draws to a close. The point of the dinner conversation was to share thoughts, ideas, experiences, worries. But now they just want to be together, to enjoy one another's company. No words are needed.

That is the nature of contemplative prayer: simply enjoying our friendship with God. It may be entirely silent, it may not. We may pray for hours or scant minutes. The difference is not in these externals but in the focus of the prayer itself. Our attention is on presence, not conversation; on God himself, not on the prayer.

There are no special readings to work through at the end of this chapter. The whole of Scripture constantly seeks to offer us the gift of this presence. It attracts and entices us, informs and stimulates us, corrects and guides us, always so that it can draw us closer to the divine author, God who has breathed his life and Spirit into the text. We hear the voice and sense its power. We see that there is something undeniably unique about this book, as peculiar as a bush that burns without being consumed. We hear words that speak of the history of God's people, of God's compassionate salvation, of liberation, of a new life. But among the words and pages we begin to sense something more: the presence of the one who speaks. And in the end, this is the foundational message of Scripture: take off your shoes; you are on holy ground.

In the Divine Presence

The crumbling Victorian church had largely been stripped of its furnishings. The darkly stained pitch-pine pews still stretched themselves across the broad distance from aisle to wall; a tall, imposing pulpit seemed to lean against one stout pillar; solemn stone monuments clung to the walls like stubborn limpets. Weak winter sunlight brought a pale, diffused glow to the deep blues and reds in the stained glass. But the interior of the church was warmed by the lively, dancing light of hundreds of flickering candles ranged across the east wall: candles tall and short, guttering and bright burning, some in glass holders of red or blue. Among the flames knelt a figure, bent over and utterly still, deep in prayer.

I was visiting the Little Brothers of Nazareth in Bristol, a city in southwest England. The Little Brothers are one of the smallest religious orders in the Catholic church. When I arrived, I asked the brother who greeted me how many brothers there were in all. "Just three," he answered. I apologized for not being clearer. "Not how many here in Bristol," I clarified; "I wondered how many of you there are around the world." He offered me a tired smile. "Yes, I understood. Just three."

The brother showed me around their center for the homeless. He was dressed in a traditional monk's habit—traditional, that is, except for being made from blue denim. He noticed my questioning look and must have been used to it. "We're a working order," he explained, "so we need a hard-wearing habit." I quickly came to understand what he meant. As we walked around the extensive center, I saw day rooms where homeless people could gather, talk and eat. We looked around the night shelter. There were showers, kitchens and offices where people could get help with welfare benefits and finding places to stay or live. An army of volunteers scurried around us as we talked. It was an extensive operation.

Finally, we walked the short distance across to the church. A former Anglican parish church, it had finally been declared redundant after the local population had moved out from the city center into the suburbs, and the congregation had slowly dwindled into oblivion. The brothers had offered to take it over as the heart of their community life, and to run it as a Catholic parish alongside their ministry to the homeless. The sense of the presence of God inside was palpable; I stood in silence for a few moments just drinking it in. The brother who was accompanying me stepped forward as though to show me around. I stopped him. "Look, perhaps we should come back," I said, gesturing toward the lone figure among the candles. "Someone's praying here right now." He smiled again. "There's always someone praying here," he answered.

And then he explained. The Little Brothers centered their life on perpetual adoration of the blessed sacrament. Which, for those unfamiliar with the Catholic tradition, roughly translates to a practice of 24/7 loving prayer in the presence of Christ, a prayer which finds its focus in the bread and wine of the Eucharist. Every hour, day and night, someone was in that church practicing the presence of God. Sometimes it would be a volunteer from the center or a worshiper from the church, but almost always it was one or other of the brothers.

I stopped him. "Wait a minute," I objected. "There are only three of you. That means each of you would have to spend around eight hours every day in here." "That's right," he replied. "But how is that possible?" I asked, amazed. "How can you do all this? How can you run this center, raise all the money you need, coordinate those volunteers, run a parish—how can only three of you do all this when you spend so much time in contemplation?"

He answered me very softly and quietly. "My friend, how do you think we could have done all this *unless* we spent so much time in contemplation?"

We walked a little way down the aisle together and moved into one of the pews. The candles flickered gently while silence wrapped around us and settled into our hearts. And, for a while, we sat with God.

EPILOGUE

Where do we go from here?

There were no readings at the end of the last chapter. From here on, our reading is the whole of the Bible. Of course, this still might seem impossibly daunting, so as you launch into the great and wonderful universe of Scripture, perhaps you might let me offer three last thoughts.

Be selective in your reading. You might find it helpful to spend a few months reading nothing but the Gospels; they may be more fruitful at first than other parts of Scripture. There is no need for anxiety about this. It seems likely that the resurrection narratives will always have more impact on most of us than the Levitical laws about mildew in houses. Most people find themselves spending more time in the Gospels, the New Testament letters, the Psalms and certain of the prophets than in Numbers, 1 Chronicles or Lamentations. It's perfectly fine to do this. As long as we're not *avoiding* any part of Scripture—as long as we're always open to the possibility of God meeting us in any part of this huge and wonderful book—there is nothing wrong with investing ourselves more heavily in those parts which most readily help us pray, love and serve.

Don't be rushed. There are any number of Bible reading plans out there that will sweep you through the book in record time—the New Testament in a year, the whole Bible in a year, the Bible in ninety days. These sprints through Scripture have some value in giving us a quick overview of the entire narrative; in the end, they can help us read the Bible more deeply. But in themselves they don't encourage good, prayerful, engaged reading. By all means use them to grasp the big picture. But then *slow down*. After you've sped through a thousand pages in three months, or a year, pick a good page or two and live with it for the next three months (or a year). Respect the fact that this is holy ground. Dwell, don't dash.

And finally, be attentive to Christ. Never lose sight of the fact that the Bible exists to draw you beyond itself into the presence of Jesus. He longs for you, yearns for you, desires you. Read like a lover. Allow your desire and longing to draw you to him. Don't be afraid.

As you open the Bible, Jesus is present. If your reading leads you to him, you're doing it right.

ACKNOWLEDGMENTS

This book is an attempt to whisper on the fringes of the Great Conversation about life in God, a conversation which has been taking place, if not since the dawn of time, at least since the dawn of writing and literature. At the very center of this conversation stands Jesus Christ, the greatest teacher and spiritual master. Around him gather towering figures, alluded to in these pages, such as the apostle Paul, Augustine of Hippo, Bernard of Clairvaux, Francis of Assisi, Teresa of Ávila, Thomas Aquinas and Ignatius Loyola. These people, and others like them, have profoundly influenced Western civilization and shaped the way most contemporary Christians follow Christ, whether we recognize it or not.

Only a fool approaches this conversation alone. These are some of the greatest minds, and most passionately devoted souls, history has yet seen. Those of us who gather at the margins to listen in, and perhaps share with one another our meager gleanings, are wise to do so in community. As I have explored the ideas and experiences described in this book, I have had the good fortune of being surrounded by people who have helped me think more deeply, live more fully and pray more richly. There are misphrasings, lacunae, simple errors here that I can proudly claim as "all my own work." But wherever this book is good, right and helpful, you can be sure you are feeling the influence of the wider circle of those who share my life, thought and prayer.

My dear friends and colleagues at Renovaré have contributed so much toward this book. Richard Foster has been a constant guide and companion. Margaret Campbell and James Catford, together with the rest of our board and ministry team, have tirelessly supported my efforts and carved out a great deal of time and space from my working life to ensure the project could be completed. We are so many, and I'm sure they will forgive me if I don't mention everyone by name. I would like, though, particularly to acknowledge Bill Vaswig, a founding member of our board and a beloved friend of us all, who so encouraged me to write, but sadly passed away before the book was completed.

The staff at Renovaré have lived with this book almost as much as I have—which is to say, probably far too much. They have borne the burden of our ministry's work while I have been secluded in libraries and studies, typing away; special thanks are due to Lyle Smith Graybeal, Joan Skulley and Mickey Cox. I'm also grateful to all those who have attended Renovaré events where I've explored and developed these ideas through conferences and retreats.

Almost everyone at Castle Oaks Covenant Church, in Castle Rock, Colorado, has helped in the process of developing these ideas, whether they were aware of it or not. Both the founding pastor, Herb Frost, and the current pastor, Paul Lessard, have become great friends and thoughtful partners in conversation. And it's been stimulating to explore the practices of *lectio divina* and silence with the members of the church's nascent contemplative prayer group; I'm especially thankful there for Chris Simpson.

My brothers and sisters in St. Dunstan's Abbey, a community of the Grey Robe Monks of St. Benedict, have shared their deepest prayer and *lectio* with me. Their impact on my own thought and formation has been inexpressible, and I'm grateful to them all.

The team at IVP has been wonderfully supportive of this project from beginning to end; no author could ask for more. I'm especially thankful for Cindy Bunch, my editor, who took some interesting ideas I had tossed onto paper and helped turn it into a *book* someone might actually want to read. Kathy Helmers, my agent, has been unstintingly encouraging, for which I am deeply grateful.

The good people of the churches in Llanfair Caereinion, Llanllugan and Manafon have, in particular, graciously explored with me many of the practices described in these pages. Three friends, Nick and Jane James, and Rebecca Reading, read a good deal of this material and offered very helpful responses.

My children—Benedict, Bethan, Francis and Gregory—have patiently borne with my absences, tiredness and occasional crankiness. They have been nothing less than enthusiastic about the project from start to finish, which still amazes and delights me. Above all, I'm grateful to my wife, Sally, my kindest (but most honest) critic and always my closest friend.

NOTES

Chapter 1: Hear His Voice

p. 13   "One dark night, fired with love's urgent longings": John of the Cross, *The Collected Works of St. John of the Cross*, trans. Kieran Kavanaugh and Otilio Rodriguez, rev. ed. (Washington, D.C.: ICS Publications, 1991), p. 358.

p. 14   "O Lord, open thou our lips": *The Book of Common Prayer and Administration of the Sacraments 1662* (Cambridge: Cambridge University Press, 2004), p. 19.

p. 14   "O come, let us sing unto the Lord": Winfred Douglas, ed., *The Monastic Diurnal* (London: Oxford University Press, 1932, 1963), p. 82*.

pp. 14-15   "There are those who always fast to read the Gospel": Matthew the Poor (Matta el-Meskeen), *The Community of Love* (New York: St. Vladimir's Seminary Press, 1984), p. 37.

p. 16   "This is what I want!": Francis of Assisi, *Francis of Assisi: Early Documents*, vol. 1: *The Saint*, ed. Regis J. Armstrong et al. (New York: New City Press, 1999), pp. 201-2.

p. 16   "follow the teaching and footprints of our Lord Jesus Christ": Ibid., pp. 63-64.

p. 17   "Pilgrim, swept by storms and weary": Alan Gaunt and Alan Luff, *Hymns and Letters: Ann Griffiths* (London: Stainer & Bell, 1999), p. 9.

Chapter 2: Learning to Read Again

p. 28   "I am the captain of my soul": W. E. Henley, "Invictus," in *The Golden Treasury*, ed. Francis Palgrave (London: Oxford University Press, 1941), p. 476.

Chapter 4: The Yearning of God

p. 52   "for example of life and instruction of manners": article 6 of the Thirty-Nine Articles in the Church of England, *The Book of Common Prayer and Administration of the Sacraments 1662* (Cambridge: Cambridge University Press, 2004), p. 613.

p. 54   "Listen carefully, my son, to the master's instructions": *RB 1980: The Rule of St. Benedict in Latin and English with Notes*, ed. Timothy Fry et al. (Collegeville, Minn.: Liturgical Press, 1981), p. 157.

Chapter 5: My Beloved Speaks

p. 66   "He also stands behind the wall": Bernard of Clairvaux, *Bernard of Clairvaux: On the Song of Songs*, trans. Kilian Walsh and Irene Edmonds (Kalamazoo, Mich.: Cistercian, 1979), 3:89-90.

p. 67   "He says, 'Arise, make haste, my love, my dove, my beautiful one' ": Ibid., p. 97.

Chapter 7: Anatomy of the Soul

p. 85   *animi extensio in Deum per amoris desiderium:* Jean Gerson, cited in William Ralph Inge, *Christian Mysticism* (London: Methuen, 1899), p. 335. Inge attributes the saying to Bonaventure (who would certainly have found it congenial), but it appears to be original to Gerson.

Chapter 8: Listen!

p. 96   "The spot was by a powerful stream called the Rie": Walter Daniel, *Walter Daniel: The Life of Aelred of Rievaulx*, trans. F. M. Powicke (Kalamazoo, Mich.: Cistercian, 1954), p. 98.

p. 99   "Listen carefully, my son, to the master's instructions": *RB 1980: The Rule of St. Benedict in Latin and English with Notes*, ed. Timothy Fry et al. (Collegeville, Minn.: Liturgical Press, 1981), p. 157.

p. 100   "All guests who present themselves are to be welcomed as Christ": Ibid., p. 255.

p. 108   "In several books I found different methods to approach God": Brother Lawrence, *The Practice of the Presence of God*, trans. Salvatore Sciurba (Washington, D.C.: ICS Publications), p. 75.

Chapter 9: Living in the Gospel

p. 118   "exactly as one friend speaks to another": Ignatius Loyola, *The*

Spiritual Exercises of St. Ignatius, trans. Louis J. Puhl (Chicago: Loyola Press, 1951), p. 28.

Chapter 10: The Book of Christ

p. 133   "remember that God speaks only a single word": Augustine of Hippo, *Ennartiones in Psalmos, In Psalmum CIII*, 4.1, in *Patrologia Latina* 37, ed. J. P. Migne (Paris: Migne, 1845), col. 1378. My translation. Augustine's original reads: "Meminit . . . cum sit unus sermo Dei in Scripturis omnibus dilatatus, et per multa ora sanctorum unum Verbum sonet, quod cum sit in principio Deus apud Deum, ibi no habet syllabas."

p. 133   "All sacred Scripture is but one book": Hugh of St. Victor, *De Arca Noe* 2.8, quoted in *Catechism of the Catholic Church*, par. 134 (New York: Doubleday, 1995), p. 43.

Chapter 11: Sacred Reading

p. 145   "*Lettera gesta docet / quid credas allegoria*": Henri de Lubac, *Medieval Exegesis: The Four Senses of Scripture* (Edinburgh: T & T Clark, 1998), 1:271 n. 1. (The loose translation in this text is mine.)

p. 147   "One day when I was busy working with my hands": Guigo II, *Guigo II: The Ladder of Monks and Twelve Meditations*, ed. Edmund Colledge and James Walsh (Kalamazoo, Mich.: Cistercian Publications, 1979), pp. 67-68.

p. 147   "the careful study of the Scriptures": Ibid., p. 68.

p. 147   "the foundation; it provides the subject matter": Ibid., p. 79.

p. 147   "puts food whole into the mouth": Ibid., p. 69.

p. 147   "the busy application of the mind to seek": Ibid., p. 68.

p. 148   "prayer is the heart's devoted turning to God": Ibid.

p. 148   "So the soul, seeing it cannot attain by itself to that sweetness": Ibid., pp. 72-73.

p. 148   "Contemplation is when the mind is in some sort lifted up": Ibid., p. 68.

Chapter 12: The Disordered Soul

p. 154   "turning away from our last end which is God": Thomas Aquinas, *Summa Theologica*, I-II.77.8, resp. (Notre Dame, Ind.: Ave Maria Press, 1981), 2:940.

p. 155   "discusses the root and origin of sin": see further Aquinas, *Summa Theologica*, I-II.84.1, 2, pp. 962-64.

Chapter 13: A Life Desired

p. 166   "We are half-hearted creatures, fooling about": C. S. Lewis, *The Weight of Glory* (New York: HarperOne, 2001), p.26.

p. 168   "The soul, . . . seeing that it cannot attain by itself to that sweetness": Guigo II, *Guigo II: The Ladder of Monks and Twelve Meditations*, ed. Edmund Colledge and James Walsh (Kalamazoo, Mich.: Cistercian Publications, 1979), pp. 72-73.

p. 170   "We cannot by direct effort make ourselves": Richard Foster et al., eds., *The Life with God Bible* (New York: HarperCollins, 2005), p. xxxiv.

Chapter 14: Beyond the Bible

p. 176   "Our gracious Queen": Edward C. Ratcliff, *The Coronation Service of Her Majesty Queen Elizabeth II* (Cambridge: Cambridge University Press, 1953), p. 39.

p. 178   "Christ has no body now but yours": see, for example, James C. Howell, *Introducing Christianity: Exploring the Bible, Faith, and Life* (Louisville: Westminster John Knox Press, 2009), p. 151.

What is Renovaré?

Renovaré USA is a nonprofit Christian organization that models, resources, and advocates fullness of life with God experienced, by grace, through the spiritual practices of Jesus and of the historical Church. We imagine a world in which people's lives flourish as they increasingly become like Jesus.

Through personal relationships, conferences and retreats, written and web-based resources, church consultations, and other means, Renovaré USA pursues these core ideas:

- *Life with God* - The aim of God in history is the creation of an all-inclusive community of loving persons with God himself at the center of this community as its prime Sustainer and most glorious Inhabitant.

- *The Availability of God's Kingdom* - Salvation is life in the kingdom of God through Jesus Christ. We can experience genuine, substantive life in this kingdom, beginning now and continuing through all eternity.

- *The Necessity of Grace* - We are utterly dependent upon Jesus Christ, our ever-living Savior, Teacher, Lord, and Friend for genuine spiritual transformation.

- *The Means of Grace* - Amongst the variety of ways God has given for us to be open to his transforming grace, we recognize the crucial importance of intentional spiritual practices and disciplines (such as prayer, service, or fasting).

- *A Balanced Vision of Life in Christ* - We seek to embrace the abundant life of Jesus in all its fullness: contemplative, holiness, charismatic, social justice, evangelical, and incarnational.

- *A Practical Strategy for Spiritual Formation* - Spiritual friendship is an essential part of our growth in Christlikeness. We encourage the creation of Spiritual Formation Groups as a solid foundation for mutual support and nurture.

- *The Centrality of Scripture* - We immerse ourselves in the Bible: it is the great revelation of God's purposes in history, a sure guide for growth into Christlikeness, and an ever rich resource for our spiritual formation.

- *The Value of the Christian Tradition* - We are engaged in the historical "Great Conversation" on spiritual formation developed from Scripture by the Church's classical spiritual writings.

Christian in commitment, ecumenical in breadth, and international in scope, Renovaré USA helps us in becoming like Jesus. The Renovaré Covenant succinctly communicates our hope for all those who look to him for life:

> In utter dependence upon Jesus Christ as my ever-living
> Savior, Teacher, Lord, and Friend,
> I will seek continual renewal through:
> • spiritual exercises • spiritual gifts • acts of service

RENOVARÉ

Renovaré USA
8 Inverness Drive East, Suite 102 • Englewood, CO, 80112 USA • 303-792-0152
www.renovare.us

formatio

TRADITION. EXPERIENCE.
TRANSFORMATION.

Formatio books from InterVarsity Press follow the rich tradition of the church in the journey of spiritual formation. These books are not merely about being informed, but about being transformed by Christ and conformed to his image. Formatio stands in InterVarsity Press's evangelical publishing tradition by integrating God's Word with spiritual practice and by prompting readers to move from inward change to outward witness. InterVarsity Press uses the chambered nautilus for Formatio, a symbol of spiritual formation because of its continual spiral journey outward as it moves from its center. We believe that each of us is made with a deep desire to be in God's presence. Formatio books help us to fulfill our deepest desires and to become our true selves in light of God's grace.